HOW TO CLEAN
EVERYTHING

Ann Russell

HOW TO CLEAN EVERYTHING

This book contains the advice and views of the author.
Readers should always consult the manufacturer before trying out any
new cleaning product or technique. The author and publisher are not liable
for any losses or damage arising from the contents of this book.

First published in 2022 by
HEADLINE HOME
an imprint of HEADLINE PUBLISHING GROUP

5

Cataloguing in Publication Data is available from the British Library

Hardback ISBN 978 1 4722 9623 8
eISBN 978 1 4722 9624 5

Designed and typeset by EM&EN
Printed and bound in Great Britain by Clays Ltd, Elcograf S.p.A.

FSC
www.fsc.org

MIX
Paper from
responsible sources
FSC® C104740

Headline's policy is to use papers that are natural, renewable and recyclable
products and made from wood grown in well-managed forests and other controlled
sources. The logging and manufacturing processes are expected to conform to
the environmental regulations of the country of origin.

HEADLINE PUBLISHING GROUP
An Hachette UK Company
Carmelite House
50 Victoria Embankment
London EC4Y 0DZ

www.headline.co.uk
www.hachette.co.uk

Contents

FOREWORD

I have been on TikTok for just over a year at the time of writing, giving advice about cleaning. Throughout this time, people have frequently asked if I could put everything in a book so they could have it to hand when needed.

I hope that whether you are a fledgling who has only just flown the nest or a seasoned housekeeper, you will find something of use. I try to cover the basics to teach those who have very little understanding, as well as tackle some more complicated tasks. No matter how experienced you are, it's always interesting to see how others do it. I learn new things every day!

The quick fixes featured at the beginning of every room are ones I have found invaluable when you have no time to clean properly and guests arriving in 30 minutes.

All mistakes are my own, and please remember I am not infallible! If your family goes about anything in a different way, and it works for you, then it is the method you should use. Cleaning is influenced by so much – climate, culture, money and personal taste. This is merely how I have found it easiest.

I also must acknowledge that I have been lucky. I was born into a first-world nation in the latter half of the 20th century, and as a result of my education and skin colour, I have been able to navigate the difficulties of life with the confidence of belonging. The only thing I have lacked is money. I try to be as inclusive as possible, but I am aware that I have blind spots. I try, but I am sure I fail sometimes, so in advance, I apologise and promise I will try to be better when I get it wrong.

I have been cleaning professionally for nearly twenty years, not a considered career choice, but one that was available and manageable with children. I have been incredibly lucky. Most of my original clients are still with me, or I with them, depending on your perspective. Many things I have learned on the job, I have had to refine how I do things, and I've made plenty of mistakes, although luckily very few were irretrievable.

TO BEGIN

The most important thing I can say is that there is no moral value to being clean, the only thing we can say about someone who has a spotless house is that they have a spotless house. There is a balance and a point at which messy and a bit grubby tips into unhealthy squalor, but the shame around cleaning and mess prevents some people who desperately need and want help, from asking for it. Hoarding is a mental illness, not a moral failing.

There is a history behind the idea of cleanliness and godliness; the idea has been used to demonise the poor and different castes and ethnicities for centuries. I cannot see the value of delving into that here – suffice to say that it is an unpleasant association and one that is not of benefit to anyone.

Despite a relentless stream of social media posts about dismantling your loo to clean it, it is perfectly possible to have a pleasant and clean living space without a huge amount of work. Very few people have spotless houses, they are busy living their lives – a few germs won't hurt you, in fact, it's been suggested they may be beneficial. We need our homes to be clean enough, not sterile, so as long as your home feels comfortable and safe for you, then it is good enough. Do not allow yourself to be shamed or bullied by people because they prefer a different surrounding. That applies whichever end of the spectrum you sit at!

Remember, the cleaning industry is worth a lot of money and a vast fortune is spent trying to convince you to buy products that won't make your life any better. The people who design these campaigns have huge budgets and they are very good at what they do – it's why many of them earn such enormous salaries.

I was told many years ago that all advertising works the same, telling you that you are ugly, old, stupid and useless. Your house smells, you can't cook, your dog is unhealthy and your children are unhappy, but if you buy product X at least one of those problems will be solved. The problem is, most people are very good indeed at taking on board the first bit, but terribly bad at remembering which product to buy. Skin cream won't stop you ageing and the most expensive air freshener in the world won't do anything except make your house smell of scent.

It won't make you happy, it might temporarily make you feel a little better, but in 20 minutes you will have become nose blind and be unable to smell it. Do what works for you, be that neat, tidy and dust-free, or having a path through the washing to the bed – both are valid, both are okay.

However, if you rent, it means you have a deposit. The structure does not belong to you and your landlord expects you to take care of it. Some landlords are excellent and are both prompt with repairs and fair and courteous in all their dealings. Sadly, many are truly awful people, who do the bare minimum they can and flout the law at every opportunity. No matter which kind you are renting from, knowing how to keep your living space clean and pleasant will help in getting that deposit back. I recommend that every interaction you have with either your landlord or their agent is done by email and those emails kept in a separate folder in case you need to prove anything agreed or requested.

Here, I will give a few hard and fast rules simply to keep you safe – the first one being to NEVER EVER mix bleach, acid or ammonia. In fact, be very cautious mixing stuff in general. Very often it's perfectly safe, but if it's not, you can make yourself very ill. People have died from mixing bleach with loo cleaner – because some loo cleaners contain either an acid or another oxidising agent, and in a confined space you can gas yourself. I've never personally exploded a loo, but I am told it has happened.

The other reason is that you can turn two useful cleaning agents into nothing but fizz (the combo of vinegar and bicarbonate of soda is a prime example) – so try to work out what you are trying to achieve and how the stuff you are using will help you. Remember there are only so many chemicals available to manufacture cleaning products, so many are just variations on a theme.

Commercial stuff is sometimes stronger and very often lacks the scent or appeal of things made for domestic use, so try not to be swayed too much by colour and scent. By all means buy what pleases you, but some very effective products don't smell very good at all. Equally, some beautifully scented stuff is actually useless at removing dirt.

Please, please, please do not use products for things they were not intended for – fabric conditioner should never be smeared on walls or skirting boards, it's flammable for a start. It's also worth checking about animals; birds, for example, are extremely sensitive to fragrances, and spray air fresheners can cause a great deal of harm. The idea that our home must be scented is one promoted to sell air freshener. A clean home should smell of very little; a bowl of dried lavender to trail a hand through in the hall can be delightful, subtle and free of harm. Free, too, if you have a lavender bush in your garden.

PRODUCTS

If you are absolutely broke, you can do most jobs with a bag of soda crystals and an old T-shirt. The soda crystals will also clean your clothes, although they are not great for stains. It's my number one product, as it has loads of uses, and while I do use laundry detergent, a spoonful

of washing soda in the drum softens the
water, meaning I only use the smallest dose
of detergent. It's great as a weekly drain treatment, too, just chuck a mugful into your sink
and follow with a kettleful of boiling water. If
you cannot find or do not have Sugar Soap
(see page 22), it is excellent for washing
surfaces and degreasing almost anything.
Wear gloves when using it as all degreasers
strip the coating from your hands and can
leave them very sore.

Dustpans, Brushes and Brooms

Having mentioned them, they deserve a word. You can
often buy a cheap dustpan and brush for a pound or so;
sometimes you will see that you have a choice
of a soft bristled brush or a hard bristled one.
A soft brush is what you want for sweeping
dust and fine particles from a hard floor.
Carpets and rugs need stiff bristles. If
you see brushes with rubber bristles,
then I advise you to grab them. They
are excellent at removing hair and fur
from carpets, but also manage fine

bits in the hallway. They are easy to wash under the tap and cope fairly well with sweeping damp things, too.

Deck Scrubs

I wasn't sure where to put this, in brooms, or mops. So it got its own paragraph. A deck scrub is a small scrubbing brush fitted to a broom handle. Essential if you have textured floors or are scrubbing your patio. The head should be replaceable, so when it starts getting soft and worn, replace it with a new one and relegate the old one to dirty jobs that don't need a handle.

Mops

I'm sure you are all familiar with the cotton mop head that squeezes out on a conical strainer arrangement over a bucket – you can get these for a few pounds almost anywhere. They are a cheap and versatile all-rounder, they don't perform as well as some of the other mops, but unless you have a large area to mop, will do fine. Do not forget to wash the heads when they get dirty. The string does tangle in the machine, so I tie it into four or five ponytails to prevent that. Or buy the ones with flat, synthetic strands on them.

There are the mops that use a roller arrangement to squeeze water out. I'm not a fan of these at all as I don't think they get the floor dry enough, and they don't go under small gaps. But some people love them. Do not confuse these with the flat Kentucky mops used commercially – they are rollered dry by a roller on the bucket and can be bought in several weights. I use the heaviest possible head to mop the floor of a large public building I clean and it works perfectly.

There is a kind of wringer mop (I used to refer to them as Dutch Mops) and you wring the head by twisting it on the handle. However, the only ones I have seen recently do not have replacement heads and thus are intended to be thrown away when dirty. That seems a shocking waste of both money and resources, but if you do see them with replacement heads, buy them plus several heads, as they work very well indeed.

I prefer to use a spin mop – there is a proprietary brand that makes them triangular and they are excellent, but the heads are expensive. I buy the generic circular ones, as the heads are cheap and easy to buy. You use centrifugal force to spin the water out using the wringer attachment in the bucket, and you can get the mop head very dry indeed. They make mopping up a spill or leak really easy, and are good for damp-dusting a floor unsuitable for free water.

Try to avoid gimmicks, though. Mop heads should be changed when dirty and a good one should be washable in the machine with all your other cleaning cloths. If you do use the cotton ones, a metal fitting should mean they are compostable, so don't put them in the bin until you've checked.

Washing Up Liquid

This is the detergent liquid used to wash dishes by hand, known as dish soap in America. It's cheap and cheerful and available in a wide range of smells and colours. I've found the really budget ones aren't very effective, so if you always wash up by hand you may find they are a false economy. I use an eco-version and buy a 5-litre container, then top up the small bottle by my sink when needed. If you have a spray bottle you can fill it with water, squirt a small amount of washing up liquid into it and use for kitchen spray. It has 101 uses, from floor cleaning to general purpose cleaning. Do NOT put it in a dishwasher or an automatic washing machine though – it produces far too much foam and you may end up with suds filling your kitchen or utility room. In soft water areas, it will do wonderfully for cleaning virtually everything, but it's less effective in hard water areas.

Spray Cleaners

These are really useful. Not because they contain a magic ingredient, but mostly because of the spray. You can cover a surface with a thin film of product and leave it to soften the dirt, then come back 5 minutes later and wipe away. I often just top up a spray bottle with water, a teaspoon of washing up liquid and (if I remember) a little white vinegar.

Anti-bacterial Sprays and Viricides

Since the advent of Covid, more and more cleaners are advertised as viricides. The most important things to remember about any of these is that they all have a contact time. If you read the small print, it will tell you how long the liquid must be left on a surface in order for it to actually achieve the results advertised. In some cases, this may be as long as 5 minutes. I find them useful to clean the exterior of loos and loo seats – drench the outside in one of these, leave while you clean the inside, then use loo roll to wipe the cleaner and dirt off, then drop into the pan and flush away. Always use loo roll for this as it disintegrates when in water and therefore flushes away without clogging your drain.

White Vinegar

I use this rather than spray polish. Most of my furniture is antique, so I prefer to use hard wax polish once a year and buff up with a spritz of white vinegar in between. Any alkali turns hard woods black, so this works more safely than water. The smell really doesn't linger. Vinegar is mildly acidic so can help to keep limescale down, but in really hard water areas it doesn't do a lot to actually remove it. It also acts as a mild anti-bacterial agent.

Window Cleaners

Mostly sold as a spray, although I think the old-fashioned pink type is still available. They are usually a mix of water, alcohol or vinegar and a mild detergent. They are formulated to evaporate quickly to avoid smears and are best used with a spotlessly clean microfibre cloth. I use them more on kitchen appliances than I do on glass. I usually use hot soapy water and a squeegee on glass, but as long as they are cheap, they are useful to have at hand.

Oven Cleaners

Most oven cleaners are simply a caustic (highly alkaline) product that eats into the brown fatty staining. They come as sprays, foams, gels, and even a bag, which you use to bathe the shelves in. Depending on how strong they are, they are remarkably effective, but can give you a nasty burn, so do wear gloves. As an important side note – alkalis turn hard woods black. If you spill caustic oven cleaner on a hardwood floor, you will see it turns blue-black quite quickly. You can bring it back with an acid, but it always shows, so just be aware and put newspaper down on the floor if using an oven cleaner.

Some of the paste scourers are useful for oven cleaning and there are a few non-caustic sprays around. They claim to give great results, but I'm not quite sure they are referring to ovens as I have always found them pretty useless.

If your oven or grill is truly black, then I recommend using the ammonia method I explain in the section on kitchen cleaning (see page 57).

Cloths

The variety of cloths to buy can be a little daunting, and the cost can be well over a fiver for a single Ecloth, and as little as 20p each for a cheap dishcloth. While I agree that for many things microfibre cloths are great, I worry about microplastics, and for some jobs the microfibre cloths are fairly poor performers – I prefer a cotton cloth in the kitchen, for example. I would buy a packet of cheap cotton cloths and possibly a glass cloth.

The yellow fluffy dusters that are everywhere are usually better after they have been washed a few times (and be aware that the yellow dye will turn anything washed with them a rather bilious yellow colour).

Cotton dishcloths – many are simply short lengths of cotton stockinette, others are a loosely woven cloth. Both are absorbent and washable, with the added bonus of being compostable when they finally die. Do read the label though, as some are not cotton but mixed fibres and do not compost completely.

You may see floor cloths as well – these are slightly larger, thicker and more robust cloths designed to clean floors and, to be honest, it's far easier to use one of these to clean a small floor than bother with a mop and bucket. If you have got a floor steamer and use it, then it is cheaper to buy a floor cloth and fold it, than buy a replacement pad. Just check the head to the steamer is able to shunt the cloth around easily.

Disposable blue cloths come either on a roll or in packets of ten or more and are quite handy for light jobs – don't forget you can wash them several times.

Wipes

Honestly? Just don't. However, if you absolutely MUST burn money, then make absolutely certain you put them in the bin not down the loo, otherwise you will get a huge bill from a plumber (as they can clog up the drains).

Scourers

Brillo pads are too fine for oven cleaning to my thinking as they get clogged too swiftly. The soft stainless steel coil scourers are far more efficient, and as they don't rust, they last much longer. If you do use a Brillo pad, cut it in half and use half at a time. Once used, they rust away within days so must be treated as disposable. They are quite useful to clean oven glass and cookware.

The sponge pads with a green or white scourer are great for washing up and light cleaning, but clog quickly with greasy stuff. They are effective in the bathroom (I write on them with a permanent marker in case I muddle them up), but once again, they are plastic so use them carefully.

There are various scratchy pads on the market, some quite expensive and some very cheap. Usually comprising a coarse knitted cover over a sponge, they are quite handy. Some people love them, but I always end up ruining them before they are truly worn out, and once again, they're plastic. If you use them with chlorine bleach, the sponge will collapse, leaving them pretty useless.

Scouring Powders and Pastes

There is a vogue at present for scouring pastes. They are tubs filled with a mix of detergent and fine pumice with a few branded extras. They are brilliant, they smell nice and they shine stainless steel to a gleam. Try using a tiny bit on your toaster – where it goes brown at the top of the slots. They are much gentler than the metal pads and I suggest you get one (choose whichever one suits your budget).

Cream cleaners are simply a more liquid version of the pastes. I must admit I quite like Cif as it has a drop of ammonia in and is great on white trainers. They are easier to rinse than the pastes, simply because they have much less pumice in them, but you may not need both.

Scouring Powders

I expect your grandmother used Vim or Ajax – again, these are both a dry powder version of the basic formula. The only one I use often is Bar Keepers Friend as it contains oxalic acid, which is fantastic at removing limescale, especially behind taps. It also brings stainless steel pans back to a shine.

When choosing between formulas, it is a very personal choice, so buy what you can afford or choose by smell as, to be honest, there isn't a lot to choose between them.

Scrapers

I keep a Stanley scraper in the kitchen. Used properly, this is invaluable for removing things from flat surfaces, but do make sure you use this held truly flat, as the blade is sharp and quite capable of gouging chunks out of a vinyl floor if not used carefully. Put it down on the surface so it lies completely flat (the blade and the end of the handle will both be touching the surface) and push firmly down and forwards. This way the edge of the blade (the sharp bit) will run across the surface rather than down into it. Holding the handle angles the blade downwards allowing it to cut into things on the surface. Start gently and get the feel of what you are doing before you do too much.

Oxygen Bleach

Now, as some of you know, I'm a big fan of the oxygen bleaches – percarbonate, peroxides, etc. They are fantastic at stain removal and get rid of blood and organic stains easily; always try them first. I do always refer to them as specifically oxygen bleach. If I refer to bleach, I mean chlorine bleach.

The one most widely known is Vanish, which comes in expensive large tubs. Cheaper ones work as well BUT the doses they give are rarely strong enough to give outstanding results. I usually chuck a mugful into a bucket with really hot water, immerse the stuff I am whitening and leave it overnight. The next day I chuck the whole lot, including the solution, into the washing machine and do a long, hot wash. This gives excellent results, but remember, once you have got things white, never wash white with anything but white.

Chlorine Bleach

This has its uses, it gets rid of some stains on white material beautifully, but splash it on dyed fabric and the only answer is to re-dye it. NEVER mix it with anything except a little washing up liquid or another known neutral agent. It's an excellent germ killer, but I rarely use it in loos as it doesn't get rid of limescale (it just whitens it), and if you mix it with other loo cleaners, it can and HAS killed people. It's easy to make a mistake. It's great at cleaning Corian and quartz, but if you overuse it, surfaces just deteriorate. I reckon it's a last-ditch effort, but it is cheap, freely available and many people swear by it.

You can mix a teaspoonful of chlorine bleach with water and put it into a spray bottle if anyone in the household has a tummy bug, as it is the recommended bactericide and viricide for things such as norovirus or C-diff (clostridium difficile), but after 24 hours, any germ-killing properties vanish. Spray it over the loo and handle, then simply leave to dry – but be aware that if it splashes on your clothes or your towels, it will take the colour out.

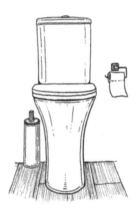

Sugar Soap

This is a strong, non-foaming detergent for washing paintwork (a similar product known as TSP is sold in the USA). It is essential prior to redecorating and is excellent at removing years of grime and cigarette tar from walls. Make it up and use as directed, and make sure you WEAR GLOVES – wash walls and paintwork down, working from top to bottom in horizontal strips to avoid run marks.

Spray Polishes

I'm sure you are all familiar with the aerosol cans of furniture polish such as Pledge. I rarely use it on wood, but on plastics around the house, it gives excellent results. It's an emulsion of water and some kind of waxy stuff, so is really good at dissolving marks on melamine and Formica surfaces; it's also handy on UPVC window frames and the like. I have seen people use it on windows, and I use it on mirrors quite often, but if light hits the glass at an oblique angle, it can look smeary. Never use it on floors unless you want a bruised coccyx!

Many supermarkets do a budget version, and unless you are wedded to the smell of a particular brand, I think they work just as well. A small shout-out to the Method spray polish, which is glycerine-based and smells lovely and almondy. It's neither better nor worse than the others, but the unusual formulation is worth mentioning; however, I don't think it works on glass.

Solid Furniture Polishes

Some of you will remember when this was the normal stuff to use. It comes in a stout, flat tin with a lever-off lid and is a blend of various waxes and a solvent that you rub on the wood surface, leave to harden a bit and then buff to a high shine. Liberon and Antiquax (as well as several other companies I can't recall at present) still make this. It can be a primary finish on wood, and after tens or hundreds of years of use, it hardens to a solid finish. It is used over French polish to give a modicum of protection and is my preferred polish for most woods.

It can be quite thick and really hard work, so I often make a very light version for monthly use. I simply grate a small block of beeswax into pure turpentine and leave it to turn into a soft paste. Beeswax on its own gives a rather sticky finish, so this allows me to clean with the turpentine while leaving behind the barest trace of wax. I like to give precious antique stuff a thorough going over once a year, both inside and out. It's a good way to check for woodworm and other damage that requires attention, and the wax finish keeps drawers sliding smoothly. The smell is an added bonus. It certainly tells people you have polished furniture.

Furniture Oils

There is a vast array of oils sold for wood. Some, such as Danish oil, are designed to be a primary finish onto bare wood; usually these have a chemical added to make the oil dry into a tough, hard layer similar to varnish. Others are designed to work as a cleaner and/or a polish – these tend not to dry but either evaporate or soak into the surface.

It's worth mentioning here that wood is dead, you cannot feed it as such but you can keep it pliable and preserved; this improves the look of the item but also increases its useful life.

Squeegees

An essential piece of kit for cleaning glass and tiles, it's the easiest way to get a smear-free finish. Wash with hot soapy water (give them a proper scrub) and squeegee off to leave a perfect shine. However, do check that the rubber blade is fairly pliable as it needs to really get all the water off and a stiff blade won't work well. Also check that the handle is at the right angle – several quite expensive ones I have used seem to have been so overdesigned they are impossible to use. Do not get a black rubber blade though, as they leave black marks on tile grout if they catch it and that can be really difficult to remove.

Melamine Sponges (aka stain erasers)

An essential bit of kit to remove marks from paint-work, these wear out quickly in use but are perfect for removing fingerprints and splashes. They do produce microplastics, so be cautious. They should be cheap though, so don't overpay – a pound shop is ideal for this kind of thing.

Rubber Gloves

A must-have. Firstly, when washing up, the water must be as hot as you can manage, so you need gloves to protect your hands from the heat. Secondly, many cleaners are really strong and will burn your skin, Sugar Soap (see page 22) being a prime example of this.

Radiator Brushes

These are stupidly useful. Buy one that is a flat strip of something with a bit of duster attached. It flexes on one plane, but is rigid on the other. I hadn't realised people didn't know about these until someone on TikTok had lost a mobile phone behind a radiator – a flat radiator brush can swoop a phone up and out in seconds, as well as keys, letters and credit cards. That alone makes it worth its cost. I have also seen the most ridiculous 'hacks' given to clean out behind radiators; one poor woman caused an explosion that burned her legs and blew a window out by spraying a highly flammable aerosol behind her radiator in order to clean away dust. It's even been suggested you pour kettlefuls of boiling water behind your radiator. Please do not do this. Buy a radiator brush – it saves a lot of trouble; mine was £2.50 at Lidl.

Spirits of Salt

For a heavily encrusted toilet, this is a must. But be aware that it will turn metal black on contact and this is not reversible. It is a very strong solution of hydrochloric acid and will burn badly, so please treat it with respect, wear gloves and keep it away from children. However, it is an extremely efficient and inexpensive chemical; it's also ideal for removing grub/food residues from concrete.

Ammonia

A very effective degreaser, I explain how to fume an oven using this in the section on kitchens (see page 57). A little ammonia with water and a drop of washing up liquid is a great kitchen degreaser. But DO NOT MIX AMMONIA with vinegar, or bleach, or any acid. It has an incredibly pungent smell, but again, it is a cheap and efficient cleaner.

White Spirit, Methylated Spirit, Isopropyl Alcohol, Acetone and Peroxide

I've lumped these together as they are all useful solvents for various marks and substances. None are terribly expensive and it's worth keeping a small amount of each to hand just in case. Some of their uses are shown in the section on stain removal.

EQUIPMENT AND APPLIANCES

Much household equipment is expensive. You can go a long way with a dustpan and brush, a broom and an airing rack, but modern appliances do make life much easier and give better results. Try to buy the best you can afford. I prefer to buy second-hand, but obviously some people would rather have new stuff. Look after it though – with a little care, these appliances should last for many years. Enhanced/extended warranties need a little investigation, so do check how much you will pay over the expected life of the machine, then see how it compares to simply buying a new one. A repairman once pointed out that for what I had paid in enhanced warranty, I could have bought two brand new machines and stored them in the garage.

Second-hand is usually a brilliant idea, but do ask to look it over before you buy anything – listen to a vacuum cleaner run, for example, to check it doesn't smell of cigarettes or make excessive noise. Local buying and selling groups are excellent for this, and for furniture as well, but do try to go to the seller's place. You will get an indicator of how they treat their belongings and, to be honest, if the seller is visibly loaded, they may well replace very serviceable stuff just because they are bored. If I offer a vacuum up for sale, it will be on its last legs and only good for spares, but I've seen virtually new fridges go up for sale just because someone with far more money than I have has decided they don't like the finish. Make sure it's clean before you part with your hard-earned cash, too. Bedbugs are rare in the UK but are making a comeback, so do be quite sure it's okay before you buy a second-hand bed or mattress – I've never actually seen a bedbug but I am told some inner-city areas are experiencing a comeback. Along with TB . . . take a minute while you contemplate that one.

After saying that, very few of the very wealthy clients I have buy new furniture. If they absolutely must, they go to Ikea. Furniture loses much of its value as soon as it is delivered. Even slightly grubby sofas can be cleaned, especially if they have loose covers. So do look for loose covers when you buy. The cover for the sofa itself will be huge and bulky – it might be too large for a domestic machine, but the cushion covers are easy to wash. A tip here is to put the washed covers on damp – avoiding the need to iron them and ensuring they fit snugly if they contract while drying – and I always put seat cushions inside bin liners before I slide the covers on – it makes it easier to get them on, but more importantly, it protects them if you spill a mug of tea! Toddlers are often leaky if they doze off on the sofa, and it is really difficult to mop a pint of pee out of a feather seat cushion.

Prevention is so much easier than cure. This is why mattress protectors and under cases exist for your bedding, as they are easy to wash. Chopping boards in the kitchen protect the work surface from cuts and burns. Rugs are put in places where spills occur (under coffee tables and

beside the bed, for example) and in front
of the fire in case of burns. Please also
remember to iron on a board, not on the
carpet. I also advise doing it near a table
in the kitchen as it is surprising how often
carpets get burned by a dropped or knocked-over
iron. If you DO wreck a carpet, it is technically possible to
patch it, but that is a tricky operation and it's incredibly
difficult to make the burn mark invisible.

If you are renting and moving around a lot, you may
not want to buy a tumble dryer. They're large and not
easy to cart around, so consider a cooling fan and
a dehumidifier. The latter MUST be a desiccant type – a
condensing one is loud, expensive and performs poorly
in the cold. As I write, a dehumidifier runs at about £170
and a fan at about a tenner, so they are considerably
cheaper as well.

Vacuum Cleaners

There are two basic types of vacuum cleaner. Cylinders,
which are things like a Henry, are great for small places,
hard floors and people in wheelchairs. They are generally more manoeuvrable. Uprights, which are better for

carpeted areas or larger places – if you have a very large place or several floors it might even pay to have one of each.

I'm reluctant to recommend brands, as every make has lovers and haters, but I do get asked about this quite often. The following are brands I have used myself.

Kirby costs as much as a car (I kid you not – check it out) but are the best vacuum cleaners for acres of carpet, however, they are really heavy and stupendously noisy, so are really not suitable for a small house or a flat.

Sebo are highly rated, as are Miele and Bosch. The ones I know are bagged machines and are well made and fairly quiet for the power. They are also rather expensive unless you manage to snag a decent second-hand model.

Dysons are Marmite for sure (love it or hate it, for those of you who don't know the advert); I personally think they peaked around the DC07 model. They are easy to dismantle, but my own experience with the battery-powered ones is that they are underwhelming but handy for crumbs.

Henry is not the best for anything, but he is solid and well made and it's a lifetime purchase. Most commercial cleaning companies in the UK use Henry machines. Make sure you use the bags though. Builders usually have one, too. If you inherit a rather battered one, I advise you to wash the white felt filter that sits between the motor housing and the bottom part from which the hose protrudes.

If you have carpets and a cylinder vacuum cleaner, you need a turbo head as it is incredibly difficult to pick up hair without a rotating brush head.

Bagless vacuum cleaners rely on the filters to maintain suction, so make sure you keep them clean. Washable filters save money, but make absolutely sure they are completely dry before you put them back in place. I find it easiest to buy a spare set, then there is no pressure to put a filter in before it is completely dry.

Cordless models are fine for a small place with hard floors, but are reliant on the battery, tend to be small and lightweight, and rarely cope with serious dirt well. Those with limited mobility may find these more accessible due to their weight. Remember, finding things that work for you and your lifestyle is as important a factor as any other.

They all need maintenance, but a little care will extend their life by years. Fill in the warranty and tape the receipt to it, then put it somewhere safe with all your other paperwork.

Carpet Cleaners

I often recommend vacuum extraction carpet cleaners. Again, they are another expensive bit of kit you may well not have the money for, but with pets and children they can be a godsend. They are another item you can find second-hand on a local buy and sell group. Being bulky, a private seller is unlikely to want to post the item. Be reasonable though – if the carpet is revolting or huge, then get a quote from a professional who has a van-mounted machine. You can often rent them – for example, my local hardware shop rents them out (some supermarkets do, too), and my editor has a 'library of things' available to rent in her local library. They are quite bulky, so if you don't have a car you may need to cadge a lift from a friend. The results they will achieve will be streets ahead of what a small domestic machine can manage.

Steamers

These range from small caddy steamers, which are very handy, to all singing, all dancing ones. They DO sanitise nicely, but are unsuitable for wood. They shoot very hot water out under pressure, so will penetrate wood fibres, causing them to swell. Depending on the water, you can easily turn hard woods black, too! I remember seeing some poor woman steaming her coffee table, showing how the dirt was coming right off. Sadly it was the finish to the wood which was being lifted by the high pressure steam. The other issue is that certain finishes are a plastic material glued onto a chipboard (or similar) carcass – many kitchen worktops are made like this. Steam is excellent to clean and sanitise the surface, but be careful not to jet it into the join. Heat often melts the glue! If you do have a laminated finish that is separating from the base, try putting a cloth pad down and ironing it to re-melt the glue, then hold it firmly in place while it dries.

I'm not keen on steamers for the floor for that reason, and also because once they have dissolved and sanitised the dirt, they rely on a small pad to pick it up. Once the fibres of the pad are clogged with dirt, they just shunt the rest around. If you do buy one, make sure you have plenty of pads, and wash them frequently.

Likewise when steaming furniture and carpets, they do a great job of sanitising them but they force dirt deeply in with the steam. Hence, this is why I prefer extraction.

The caddy ones are useful as they are superb for forcing grease and grime out from crevices and hinges where it can then be wiped away with a cloth. I like to blast oven hinges and crevices with a fine jet of steam to see what emerges.

Washing Machines

Washing machines are expensive, so if you are buying one, then absolutely comb online review sites. Check as many places as possible, understand what features they offer and think about how much you will actually use those features. I was dismayed to find a client had a lovely new Wi-Fi enabled machine with a little hatch to put that odd sock that had escaped when loading. Sadly it didn't have a way to adjust the pre-programmed settings without the phone app. I suspect a far cheaper model would have been more useful, as I cannot do a quick wash on linens, and have yet to use the little sock hatch, which I thought would be so very handy.

Most places have a washing machine as a fixture when renting, but if not, you might consider a spin dryer. Again, they are MUCH more portable than a washing machine and about a hundred quid cheaper. Washing clothes by hand isn't that hard, but getting the water out enough to dry sensibly is where it gets difficult. Wringing in a towel can be somewhat effective, but after a while you are left with a heap of damp towels to dry as well as your jeans. Pants and socks can be done in a salad spinner though, so if a spin dryer is beyond your means, take the big stuff to the launderette and do the little things at home.

TRENDS

Avoid this year's 'must-have' gadget. It's a waste of money, you'll use it furiously for a month, then it will get dumped into a cupboard until it makes its way to Oxfam. My evidence? Juicers, chocolate fondue sets, cheese fondue sets, spiralisers, Jamie Oliver's Flavour Shaker? – all fairly specific tools which just do one job. You stand a better chance with a more versatile item (but the current craze for air fryers will run out of steam eventually, although you stand more chance of getting your money's worth out of it). A microwave has become standard in most kitchens, but is not used as often as you might think by a lot of people.

ROUTINE

Depending on your mentality, cleaning can be a relaxing way to clear your mind, or a stressful and upsetting struggle. If you work or study (and even if you don't!), you may find you resent your free time being spent scrubbing the kitchen floor. If you can spend a little time each day doing the immediate tasks, then that reduces the amount of time spent doing a blitz on the place. 10–20 minutes every night and 10 minutes before you leave in the morning should keep your space under control, leaving your precious free time less encumbered by washing.

I find that when I get home I am exhausted and I have no desire to do a damn thing. If I sit down I am unlikely to get up again, and I am unlikely to even bother to eat properly, just grabbing biscuits and a gin to fill a gap before bed. Not a healthy or economic way to live, by anybody's standards.

I find the trick is to not sit down, just remove your coat or jacket and go straight in to prepare food and tidy. I race around like a rather short-tempered terrier until food is cooked, a load of washing is hung up to dry and a cursory attempt has been made at restoring order. I load and run the dishwasher and leave the rest. After I am up and awake the next day, I wipe down the kitchen and put any laundry on to wash. If I have plans for the weekend, I make an attempt to properly sort out at least the bathroom and sofa to ensure the place looks semi-respectable. It sounds more than it actually is and as long as I do that every day, I really don't fuss too much. The floor may look a bit hairy, but to be honest, I can ignore that fairly easily.

Both physical and mental health will affect your abilities. I am aware that one frequently follows the other, so please accept this as a suggestion, no more. Those who find it difficult to maintain focus may find it easier to group those small chunks by area. Start by wiping the work surface, then empty the dishwasher and empty the crumbs from the toaster. If you are still able to, sweep the floor. It's far easier to maintain focus if the jobs are in your sight.

If you are exhausted but in dire need of a bit of order, you might find that grabbing a rubbish bag and dealing with rubbish for a set period of time helps – either use a timer or put on an energising dance track. Make a deal with yourself – go thus far and no further.

If you are physically struggling, then remember you don't have to do everything. I often clean my bathroom sink while sat on the loo as it is in reach, but never feel obliged to clean the bath as well – it's not obligatory to do everything at once. If you vacuum half the living room and no more, you have still vacuumed 50 per cent of the space, so it's less to do another day.

Likewise the priorities. Dirty mugs and plates often look and smell gross, and because of that they affect how you view both the space and the task. If you deal with some of those, then you may feel more encouraged the next time you come to the mess.

If you find you get easily overwhelmed, I strongly suggest you force yourself to do at least 30 minutes of cleaning or tidying every day, broken down into two chunks for ease. It makes the world of difference, and of course, it's far easier to clean a space if it is reasonably clean and tidy to start with.

It also means if you need to have a plumber to invade your space for repairs, you won't feel quite such a slob. However, unless you are storing body fluids (please, if you feel compelled to do this, may I urge you to seek help – your GP will direct you to someone and I promise you that you can get better!), I know they will have seen it all before.

Perhaps a Regular Set of Tasks Will Help?

Monday am – Put clothes from the weekend in to wash, wash up any stuff left from the previous day. Remove food from the freezer if required for supper that day.

Monday pm – Put dinner on to cook, put clean laundry on a rack to dry, wipe kitchen worktop and bash toaster over the bin.

Tuesday am – Put loo cleaner into the bowl, clean the bathroom sink, empty the upstairs or bedroom bins.

Tuesday pm – Put dinner on to cook. Finish cleaning the loo and clean the bath or shower. Remove dry clothes from the rack, put away or fold, ready to be ironed. Rearrange clothes on the rack that are still damp.

Wednesday am – Strip bed and put it on to wash, wipe out fridge. Put rubbish ready to go to the kerb for bin day (as long as it is bin day tomorrow where you are! – adjust accordingly).

Wednesday pm – Hang wet bedding up to dry and make bed with clean linen. Put towels on to wash. Put rubbish to kerbside as required.

Thursday am – Make sure you are up-to-date with the washing up, and the laundry is put away and sorted.

Thursday pm – Tidy living room, run a duster round, then after dinner do any ironing while you watch the news.

Friday am – Tidy bedroom, check bathroom, make sure the fridge is wiped and ready for new food.

Friday pm – Do your weekly food shop on the way home and put it all away before you go out.

Hopefully this means you really only have to vacuum the floors, mop and deal with the washing from a work-week at some point over the weekend. When you have the time and energy, you can then deal with a deep clean of every room without having to deal with daily mess, too.

CLEANING BY ROOM

Before we get into each room, it's worth mentioning that none of this needs to be overwhelming. Take things one step at a time. If it takes you 2 weeks to get the rubbish bagged and out of a room, then that is how long it takes. If you do one more thing to tidy than you do to create mess, then you are on the right track. I find most tasks really tedious, so I listen to audio books while I work. I borrow mine from the library for free; I have an app on my phone. I strongly advise you to join your local library for just that reason. Some people set a timer for 10 or 20 minutes to give themselves a limit. Other people use energetic music to put them into the right frame of mind.

For each room, I've suggested the order I do for two reasons. Firstly, it should prevent you having to do the same task again and again. More importantly, you are prioritising things that make you feel bad. Untidiness and disorder do upset some people immensely but are not the same as dirt. However, rubbish and stale food smell unpleasant and attract flies and mice, so they are more important factors to consider for your health.

KITCHEN

Quick Fix

Wipe the worktop, polish up the taps, quickly clean the sink, stack washing up neatly or load the dishwasher. Hang cloths and tea towels neatly. Makes the kitchen look far better in just a few minutes.

Things You Might Not Have Tried

A folded length of kitchen paper placed in the bottom of the bin under the bin liner. Keeps smells down and keeps the bin from needing a wash as often.

A spoonful of soda crystals in the washing up water reduces the amount of washing up liquid used – wear gloves to get the water scalding hot and achieve sparkling results.

General Tips

It's a good idea to keep at least a bit of your kitchen spotless in order to prepare food. You should always use a chopping board in order to protect your worktops, especially if they are melamine or wood, and your knives, if they are quartz or granite. NEVER put a hot pan straight on the worktop either. A few solid chopping boards make life easier; you can transfer them to the sink for a scrub, wipe the surface below and put them back. I prefer wood as it won't melt if I put a pan on it, nor blunt my knives. They're easily cleaned by chucking them in the sink, scrubbing with a scrubby and washing up liquid, then rinsing under a hot tap. However, never immerse them and leave them to soak – the board will warp and come apart.

Before you go food shopping, clean out your fridge. Throw away anything that is not edible (tip – if it says hello, it needs to go in the bin), wipe the shelves down, then tidy them. It means you know what to buy, and what NOT to buy; it also means that you have space for your food when you get home.

Make a list – it's MUCH easier when you are in the super-market if you know what to buy; it also saves you money. ALWAYS have something to eat before you hit Tesco, as hunger can cost an extra £50 at the checkout. If you can manage it, make a meal plan for the week's meals. Try to make lunch to take to work or wherever you go – again, it will cost a quid or so to make lunch, but the burger van or sandwich shop can easily take eight quid off you if you are hungry.

While you are wiping out the fridge, look at the back of it – in many fridges there is a v-shaped indent running down to a hole in the middle, or a narrow channel/indent that runs across and down at an angle to one side. That hole leads to a pan on the back, which sits on top of the motor housing. It's designed so that any condensation inside the fridge runs away and evaporates off. Sometimes the hole gets blocked and you find water inside your fridge, usually under the salad drawer. If the little pokey thing isn't to hand in the hole, you can use a skewer to clear it. If your new fridge starts to smell really bad, pull it out and check as you may have left polystyrene packing in the evaporation tray!

Check your cupboards, too. It's easy to forget you still have an unopened jar of mustard at the back of your cupboard. Repeat that mistake a few times and you have enough mustard to last for several years. Take a damp cloth to the cupboard while you have a look and wipe up any sticky stuff you find. Check some things are still okay. Wholemeal flour, for example, is fattier than white and goes rancid a year or so before white flour becomes past its best.

Keep a bottle of kitchen spray to hand. If you buy a bottle with a screw-on top rather than a clip on, when you refill it you can use a little washing up liquid and either water or white vinegar. Not only does this save money, it cuts down on plastic use as well.

I like to buy cotton dishcloths (a pack of four or five is under a £1 and they last for ages). To wash them, just put in the machine along with tea towels and cleaning cloths – a good 60 degrees wash will render them clean and sanitary. Then just spray your surfaces, leave the cleaner to sit for a few minutes and wipe clean. Don't forget to wipe UNDER things and brush out your toaster, too (if you don't, you'll end up setting off the smoke alarms at 6am).

Use-by and Best-before Dates

Use-by dates on food indicate that the food may be unsafe to eat past that time. There are usually a few days margin as they factor in supply chain delays, plus the time goods are out of the fridge while restocking shelves, etc, so don't just assume. However, I must make clear here that the government food safety advice says to use food by this date, so please be careful if you choose to ignore this. Things like cream and milk taste truly nasty when they turn, and fish smells fishy and unpleasant (skate usually smells of ammonia even when fresh so don't be put off by that). Salisbury market has a cheese stall selling short or over-date coded cheese for a fraction of what supermarkets sell it for. The brie is very often still not ripe despite it being a week or two past the use-by date. Use your eyes and your nose; food waste is a massive problem and one we should all be mindful of. There are a few apps that allow retailers to sell food that is still good but needs eating quickly for a heavily discounted price, and very

often you can freeze it. There are companies who special-
ise in what they refer to as short-coded shelf-stable food,
and if you are on a tight budget, I strongly suggest you
look them up; several have online shops. The selection
can be a bit odd at first and for obvious reasons it's never
things that are sold in volume by Tesco. You can buy
the little luxuries that make life nicer, even if they have
unfamiliar names.

Best-before dates are usually on jarred or canned food
as well as packaged dry food like pasta, cereal, biscuits,
etc, and while the food may still be perfectly safe to eat
(I gather some cans are safe for decades), the quality,
flavour, colour and texture may begin to deteriorate after
this date. It's still safe to eat, but it's up to you whether
you want to or not. Sometimes nothing happens beyond
the best-before date. I'm sure you've all noticed that salt
has a best before date on it? It's not bad after this date but
it might start to clump and solidify.

Second-hand Furniture and Household Goods

Kitchen equipment is another place where second-hand
can prove to be a money saver. Many people treasure
vintage items for their rarity value. I have seen several

impressive Pyrex collections. My best dinner service (I know, I am that old) is top of the range but second-hand. I like eating from good china and it gives me pleasure to own something that would have been beyond my means at 30. When it comes to buying pans, I would rather have a mismatched set of top-quality second-hand pans than a brand new mediocre set. One pan I have has been by my side for 40 years. In fact, charity and thrift shops can be excellent places to buy all sorts of household goods – my kitchen (like the rest of my house) comprises largely of second-hand stuff I have bought for very little and it's usually a far higher quality than I could afford if I bought new. It's absolutely worth routinely checking if you are thinking of getting anything at all. After all, I'd rather pay £3.50 for a cafetière than £20. Sod's law though does say that you only find the item you have been hunting down for ages a day after you gritted your teeth and paid full price in John Lewis.

Washing Up

If you can run to it, and you have space for it, then a dishwasher is the most economic and efficient way to go. It saves on both water and electricity but it is a big upfront cost. However, keep an eye on local buy and sell groups as you often see appliances for very little money (I have already written about this so check back if you need to). Make sure you keep the salt compartment and the rinse aid topped up EVEN if you use the all-in-one tablets. Check your water hardness and set the machine accordingly – your local water supplier will have details about this. Clean the filter regularly (once a week is ideal), and the rotor arms come off, too, so check they aren't blocked. Run a cleaner through every six months or so – I buy specially made sachets from a pound shop.

If you don't have a dishwasher, then to wash up you'll need: a pair of rubber gloves, a bottle of washing up liquid, a dishcloth or scrubby sponge, a stainless steel scrubby (the soft non-scratch type) and a clean tea towel. I prefer to use a bowl as I'm less likely to break a glass, I can still empty things out into the sinks and I use less water.

Fill your bowl with HOT water (that's why you need rubber gloves, to protect your hands from the heat) – pour in a kettleful of boiling water if your water only comes out lukewarm. Start with glasses, then mugs, then bowls and plates, washing dishes and saucepans last. If the bubbles in your bowl die it means you need clean water and more washing up liquid, likewise if the water gets cold or looks manky. I rarely rinse but some people prefer to, and in fact, this only comes second to the meat washing argument for ongoing fierce online bickering. I figure I use around 5ml of washing up liquid to 5 litres of water, the vast majority of which drains away when I remove the item from the water; that is such a small amount it's not worth worrying about. But other people strenuously disagree and prefer to rinse each time.

Then leave your stuff to drain. One reason your water needs to be properly hot is that water evaporates off things quickly, meaning you hardly touch it with the tea towel before you put it away. I find if you place glasses and cups onto a clean dry tea towel to drain, any water is absorbed by the cloth and there is no need to dry at all. Hot water also means your detergent is more efficient – I always know when someone has washed up in warm water because everything has a film of grease on it.

Wash up daily, and if you must leave a pan to soak, leave it neatly by the sink, not in it, otherwise you will end up with a sink full of cold greasy water and dirty pans.

Wipe your hob every time you use it, as this makes life easier in the long run. If you drench it in kitchen spray and leave it to sit while you wash up, then any dried-on bits will have softened enough to just be easily wiped away. Once you are finished, rinse your cloths out and hang to air them – don't leave in a sodden heap to breed germs.

For a Thorough Oven and Hob Clean

If your hob is glass/ceramic, then the caustic oven cleaners work really well. Just wait until the hob is cold, then spray the marks with oven cleaner and leave for 20 minutes. The surface should just wipe clean.

Gas hobs seem a little tricky but most of it comes off. Lift up the iron pan supports and put them in a sinkful of hot soapy water, then lift off the burner bits – usually a flame regulator and a plate. Pull the knobs up and off (if it is a stand-alone cooker, you can take off all the knobs) but be careful not to lose the little metal clip inside each (they will work perfectly well without this clip but will be slightly loose). The metal post that sticks up has a flat face, which ensures the knobs go back on correctly. Now spray liberally with kitchen spray, go and wash the pan supports and burners, then come back and wipe the hob top. If the black markings wipe off, do not panic, you can buy stickers from Amazon or eBay to replace them. If you have a temperature dial on the front, I suggest you take a picture of it before you clean – this means you can ensure the sticker gives reasonably accurate temperatures if you should need to replace it with a sticker. I had the very devil of a job baking cakes after I wiped off the guides on one of our cookers and put the sticker on incorrectly.

The old-fashioned electric coils are very often either set into a top which hinges up to clean underneath, or there is a sliding tray below it that can be accessed from the grill compartment. Either way, you can put foil underneath to save cleaning but do change it regularly.

Clean your oven often – again, it makes life easier in the long run. Spray with caustic oven foam and leave for 30 minutes, then use a stainless scrubby and wipe clean. If it is encrusted and black, then use ammonia. If there are two layers of glass in the door you can usually remove the inside layer in order to clean between the two layers. Sometimes they simply slide up and out, or you unclip a bit of plastic, while others require you to unscrew two metal washers holding the glass in place. Do remember though that the glass adds weight, and once you remove it, the door may decide to swing up or across and close rather briskly.

Ammonia for Oven Cleaning

Firstly, turn the oven off and label it so no one tries to use it, as it will be out of use for 24–36 hours. Now block off any vents with a plastic bag – my fan oven gets a bin liner folded up to cover the fan vent and the shelves are pushed back to hold it in place. What you are doing is fuming the inside, so it needs to be sealed.

Then pour a bottle of household ammonia into a jug, put it in the oven, close the door and go about your business for a day or so. After the allotted time, remove the jug of ammonia (pour it back into the bottle for reuse) and start to scrub the oven and shelves – all that brown stuff will be soft and rubbery and just fall away into the water.

Ammonia has a seriously pungent smell (it was used as smelling salts when women fainted a lot in days gone by) and if you have blocked sinuses it will bite through that in a breath. It's not particularly harmful though, so just keep it away from your face and hold your breath if possible. Stand outside in the fresh air and you will soon be okay. Honestly, you'll be fine.

Cleaning the Floor

Sweep or vacuum first, then you can mop. If your kitchen has a larger floor or your knees are a problem, then use a mop (I covered different types of mop to use in an earlier chapter, see page 9). There is a type of mop which incorporates a bottle of spray cleaner into the mop itself, but it needs a LOT of pads, and you need to change the pad out as soon as it's grubby – they only absorb so much and need a wash once gunked up, but if you have limited mobility, you may well find they are easier.

If you are broke or only have a small kitchen, then just use a cloth and a bucket or bowl of hot soapy water, get down on your knees and wipe the floor. Cut-up old T-shirts (or any old cotton garment) make great cloths as they are usually tightly knitted cotton and do an excellent job. I find they last as long as all my other cloths. I recommend cutting them into neat squares before use. Cut off the seams as these are uncomfortable and get in the way when you are wiping things, and while your old pants make great dusters, it is less embarrassing if your flatmate does the dusting.

A handy tip is to use your cleaning bucket (I have several 99p flexi tubs from Poundland) as a laundry basket for household cloths and sponges. When it's full, throw the lot into the washing machine. It's a waste to throw something away when a good wash will bring it back.

Rubbish

Depending on what the disposal methods are where you live, it can be anything from a simple wheelie bin or black sack to an array of containers. The general principle still holds though. WRAP your rubbish tightly to contain smells and keep flies away as much as possible. Every Thursday morning (our bin collection day), Hollie and I argue over the bits of chicken strewn over the pavements. Foxes and cats have torn open the sacks overnight to access the food within, but if you first wrap it up tightly, either in a knotted carrier bag or in a secure newspaper parcel, then put it in the black sack, they usually won't bother. This hugely reduces the smell in hot weather and also the likelihood of maggots. It keeps your bins clean and much fresher smelling, too.

Fruit Flies

These tiny, slow-moving flies live for weeks and feed on any available source of sugary nourishment. If you have them, you can be certain there is a source of food. I actually checked; the bloody things live for a month. Check the fruit bowl, your worktops, your kitchen bin, etc. Once you are completely free of anything, they do leave, but emptying a kettleful of boiling water into the sink every night prevents any eggs hatching (it also keeps the drain fresh). Some people make traps using a little old wine or vinegar and water in a jar with a drop of washing up liquid to break the surface tension, then a tight lid of cling film with a hole in. However, I think this is a last resort because although you are trapping them, you are also attracting them. I have found that once you track down every source of food, they leave quickly enough, so it's simply a matter of checking everywhere and not just in the obvious places, for example, a shrivelled orange in the larder is easy to miss.

Grease on Cabinet Tops

If you have wall-hung cabinets you will find the top becomes coated with a layer of sticky, greasy dust. It's not doing much harm, but if you cannot ignore it now you have found it, then here is how you only need to clean it once. Spray the cabinet top(s) thickly with something like Sugar Soap (see page 22) and leave to sit for 30 minutes. Use a stainless scrubby to loosen all the gunge. Get a bowl of hot water and remove all that with a cloth. You will need to rinse it clear almost every time you wipe and may have to go over it two or three times to get it completely clean. Leave it to dry properly.

Next, get a roll of tin foil and a pair of scissors. Spray the cabinet top lightly with plain tap water. Unroll the tin foil in a length to cover the top, then smooth into place with a dry cloth. You may need to use two lengths to cover the depth of the cabinet. Now whenever you feel the urge, you simply lift the tin foil and replace it. This tip also works on vertical surfaces, so if your cooker backs onto a painted wall and gets spattered with grease, you can cover it easily.

BATHROOM AND LOO

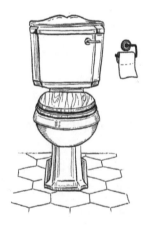

Quick Fix

Get rid of clutter, bin everything you won't be using, stand all bottles neatly upright, clean the sink, polish the taps, and put a squirt of cleaner into the loo. Wipe any visible marks. This makes the room look cleaner in just a few minutes.

Things You Might Not Have Tried

Keep a small bucket or flexi tub in a corner with the basic cleaning kit to hand. You're more likely to use it if it's close to hand.

If your bathroom mirror fogs up, then put a drop of liquid soap onto a dry cloth and polish the mirror with that – it does help.

General Tips

Pick your poison – use either bleach OR limescale remover. Only ever keep one type in the bathroom. It makes accidents less likely.

Keep a plunger near the loo, especially if you have guests. It saves embarrassment. Also, if you have guests who may be menstruating, then leave a few tampons and pads visible on the side, perhaps in a pretty bowl.

On the subject of embarrassment, if 'things' don't flush away, first try squirting a line of shower gel or similar onto them before you try flushing again. Very often this ensures the second flush works. Do NOT do a pre-emptive squirt though, otherwise the bowl may fill with foam.

For a Thorough Clean

Bathrooms are dusty places, it's all the towels, so before you do any wet cleaning, use the upholstery nozzle on your vacuum to go over every inch of it, then when you use a damp cloth you don't come away with lots of dust and hair.

The bathroom is another place where it is important to leave the cleaning fluids time to work, and if you have hard water, it is vital you use products specifically labelled for limescale removal – some claim to prevent limescale but do bugger all to remove it once it is there.

As I have mentioned before, NEVER EVER EVER mix bleach with any other bathroom product – any containing acids, ammonia or oxidising agents will react and produce an exceedingly dangerous gas. People can die from this. It is the main reason I never use bleach in the loo or bathroom. Other products work far more efficiently at cleaning and the risk of accidentally gassing yourself is higher than you might think.

If you use a product containing hydrochloric acid, it will stain metal quickly and irreversibly, so most proprietary formulations use another acid. I prefer the thicker ones rather than the foamy ones simply because they are easier to work over a surface – as you move the product around you can feel the underlying surface change from rough to smooth as the cleaner dissolves the scale.

Start by taking all the bottles of shampoo, tubes of toothpaste, etc, away from the surfaces and either pile them in the sink or put them on the floor. Then, using your cleaner, spray the shower liberally – don't forget the shower hose and head, and if it is an over/in-bath shower,

then spray the taps as well as the entire bath. If you want to take the loo seat off (some just unclip for cleaning) now is the time – just put it in the bath. If not, fear not, removal is not mandatory – remember, anywhere pee can go, so can cleaning fluid and water. If the seat doesn't come off, now is the time to spray the seat and the hinges liberally with cleaner. Spray the front and pedestal, especially at the front, and the floor immediately under.

Spray the sink and the taps, wipe surfaces down around the sink and scrub the sink. Don't forget to clean all around the taps and the underneath surface of everything, including the underside of taps and the vertical part of a hand basin (the bit in which the overflow sits). Polish up the taps and leave to dry while you tackle the bath and shower. A toothbrush is the ideal tool to get into corners and behind things, then when you feel the surface has come smooth, use the shower to rinse everything off (use your scrubby to rinse the hose, if necessary), and then use a squeegee to clean down the shower screen and bath.

Now back to the loo. Use loo roll to wipe around the rim and down the front to remove dribbles, then flush the paper. Then you can use a cloth wrung out in hot water to wipe the outside of the loo – go all around to the back, rinsing your cloth as needed until the loo is sparkling. It's a smooth, dry surface now so no smells lodge. Again, I use a permanent marker to ensure the cloth for the loo remains for the loo.

Turn your attention to the hinges – if any discoloured liquid is seeping out (and before you freak out, it's more than likely rust from the fixings), then spray. Absolutely drench the hinges, then use loo roll again to wick it away. While it runs through, lift the seat and spray – again, use loo roll to wipe as it is flushable. Wipes and kitchen paper are made to remain in one piece when wet so will cause a drain problem, whereas loo roll is made to disintegrate in water.

Once the seat is clean and dry, flush and ensure no paper is left floating in the bowl. Once you have nothing but water in the bowl, use your loo brush to push the water out. I've demonstrated this several times online but I will try to describe it here. You push the brush firmly down to push the water down and up around the bend. It will sloosh up, and then back – as it starts to go back towards the bend, you use the brush to shove it further. Work with the motion of the water and it doesn't splash. Once that's clear, you apply loo cleaner up under the rim and around where the waterline was.

Now, reassemble the bathroom, polish off marks on the outside of the shower screen and make sure the taps are gleaming. If you have a towel rail, don't forget to wipe and polish it so it sparkles. Either mop or wipe off the floor, check it all looks nice, leave the loo to soak, and have a cup of tea.

When you feel like it, flush the loo, run the brush around, then flush again. Admire your handiwork. Resolve never to despoil such a shining temple of perfection. Realise you absolutely have to pee. Never mind.

LIVING ROOM

Quick Fix

Start by opening the windows wide. Plump cushions and straighten or fold throws. Stack magazines and books neatly and vacuum the floor. Remove both rubbish and any washing up. If the sofa looks comfortable and inviting and the floor reasonably clear, then the whole room will look better. Close the windows. Spray polish or cleaner on the door and clean it – the fresh scent is then noticeable as people walk through the door. Clean any obvious mirrors.

Things You Might Not Have Tried

Ring marks on polished wood look shabby. There are various proprietary formulas that work well, my most reliable one is HG Meuballine, but the old-fashioned trick of rubbing a raw shelled nut (try walnut) dipped in fine ash (cigar ash is the one they suggest – pure snobbery) over the ring mark is effective. In a pinch, a drop of cooking oil rubbed in well sometimes does the trick.

If you have an empty space, try filling the wall with art rather than the floor with furniture. This makes the room much easier to keep clean and a carefully curated collection is very pleasing. It can upgrade your living space without creating clutter.

A collection of plants on a windowsill can give privacy without needing screens or nets.

General Tips

Curtains and upholstery hold smells due to being absorbent. If your living room smells stale or doggy, then either wash or take curtains, etc, to the cleaners. Neatly tucked-in throws are quick to wash if you have pets and can be removed in seconds if guests arrive.

People never put things on the coasters provided. I spend a lot of time wiping away ring marks when a spotless coaster is just inches away. Put trays down instead, then you just gather up the tray to clear the crockery and glasses, then replace. I have no idea why, but people who ignore the hundreds of helpful coasters dotted over furniture seem to be able to put things on a tray.

Put lightweight washable rugs down where people's feet go, and where spills happen – again, it's easier to chuck a cheap thin rug in the machine than it is to clean the entire carpet.

For a Thorough Clean

This is where you can perfect the order of things, because your living room, like your bedroom, is usually where stuff accumulates. I generally find it's easier if it's done in a certain order – as always, you may think differently here, so remember I am not an oracle, you do it your way.

Grab a rubbish sack, go around and chuck all the rubbish in, empty the bin, scrape old cauliflower cheese into it – everything. Don't tie up the sack unless it is bulging, just twist the top and put it by the door, you're bound to find other stuff as you go.

Now take all the dirty crockery and glasses out to stack by the sink. Don't attempt to wash up, unless you can load them straight into a dishwasher. You may well find other offerings behind things and you don't want to get distracted. I tend to ignore this advice and leave a trail of destruction behind me.

If this is all you can do, the place will feel a lot clearer. You can always carry on tomorrow, but if you do a tiny bit every day, it will slowly come together.

Now you can see what you are left with, so get a small bucket or bowl of hot soapy water and a cloth, and now I digress to explain why . . .

Dust

Dust is simply fine particulate matter that is thrown up into the air, only to fall slowly down onto every surface there is. If you just run a duster over every surface, most of that dust is simply knocked back into the air, only to land again an hour later.

The biggest cause of dust is smoke – from cigarettes, from candles, from incense sticks, from joints, you name it (vapes, by the way, leave a sticky film on things but no dust) – pets leave not just fur but dander everywhere, too. If you live by a busy road, then traffic grit/dust will coat your windows, work its way in and coat your furniture.

If your place is thick with dust, start by using the upholstery brush on the hose to vacuum the surfaces – it won't get it all but it does get rid of the really thick layers that build up on books, etc, and behind things. Try to vacuum around the ceiling and lights, too.

Spray polish is mostly a way to persuade the dust to stick to the duster, it smells nice and tries not to leave streaks. It kinda works, but not very well and can make your duster really claggy. It's far better to wring a cloth out in water – hard, so it's just damp – then wipe surfaces free of dust (with that in mind, I refer you back to the small bucket or bowl of hot soapy water I mentioned at the beginning of this section). Regularly dunk the cloth in the water to rinse the dirt free and into the water. Coffee cup rings and spills can easily be cleared up and you won't end up a sneezing mess; you might want to change the water every so often if it looks particularly nasty. This is known as damp dusting – all that fine stuff is now in a bowl of water so it won't be coming back any time soon.

While you are dusting, you can tidy up, put things back where they belong, a pile to go upstairs, dirty socks by the machine, more cups by the sink. If something hasn't actually got a home, put it in a tidy heap to be checked over – I find laundry baskets help here. Start high though, sweep cobwebs from the light fittings and ceiling before you dust the coffee table. It's no fun to do that twice, and even if you vacuumed, there will be cobwebs you missed.

Look at the freshly dusted furniture – if it looks a bit smeary, now is the time for spray polish and a clean duster.

Finally, you vacuum the floor. Try to pull furniture out to go under and behind, but don't beat yourself up if you can't – decent people don't check for dust behind your sofa; ask any that do to leave in a hurry. To ensure the very edge of a carpet is clean, wrap a damp cloth around your finger, then using your cloth-covered finger, shove it into the crevice between carpet and skirting board and wipe firmly. You'll be amazed at what comes up.

Put your tools away, stand back and admire your handiwork, make a cup of tea, sit down and disarrange your artfully placed cushions. Look at the ceiling and spot a large cobweb you missed. Never mind, it will keep.

BEDROOMS

Quick Fix

First, open the windows. Change pillowcases, smooth sheets and make the bed. Put any washing into the hamper, hide clutter in the wardrobe or shove under the bed. Clean the mirror and run a vacuum over the floor. Close the windows, then turn low-level lamps on and overhead lights off.

Things You Might Not Have Tried

If you are not a restless sleeper, then use a top sheet under the duvet, it's half the amount of fabric to wash and means you can buy a really lovely duvet cover and wash it twice a year. But this doesn't work well if you thrash around at night.

For those of you with awkward bunks and beds, there is an all-in-one duvet with cover version, which I believe are sold by Marks & Spencer. Americans use them and call them comforters – much to the confusion of those who use duvets. But as you can put the whole thing in the washing machine, they are much easier if you struggle with covers. Especially if your child gets inside the cover, then falls out of bed and sleeps suspended in their makeshift hammock. Which has happened to mine several times. They then wake at 5am with banshee wails of distress. Usually when you have a hangover.

Make sure your bedroom gets cold overnight. We sleep far better if the room is cooler than when we are up and about. I feel the cold terribly so I get into a pre-warmed bed and turn the electric blanket off. Then by around 11pm, the room is really quite cold. The heating then kicks in just before I awake; if not, I scramble into a thick dressing gown and slippers to warm up. Our bodies naturally drop their temperature while we sleep, as essential meatsuit maintenance proceeds, so keeping yourself too warm can interfere with this. It can be why some people sleep so badly in summer when the outside air doesn't cool off enough.

General Tips

Bedrooms can easily become a dumping ground for washing, shopping and random bits and bobs that don't have a home. As most people don't spend much time awake in their bedroom, they fail to notice how steadily it becomes a mess. That mess, however, can interfere with both your physical health and mental wellbeing. A clear and clean bedroom enables better restful sleep, and also a smoother transition into the daytime activities. Being able to access your clothes and stuff with ease allows for a more positive frame of mind. If you struggle with organisation, try using large shopping bags or tubs, or laundry baskets. It keeps things off the floor, keeps a certain amount of organisation while keeping things in sight. The biggest problem people have with mess is the inability to find things, so when they dive in they create more mess. Having visible categories helps!

For a Thorough Clean

First, grab a bin liner and do the rubbish, then clean any crockery and glasses/mugs, etc. I would open the window, too, and get some fresh air into the bed. Decide if your bed linen needs a complete change – if not, then clean pillowcases and possibly a bottom sheet will go a long way to making it feel fresher.

Before you start dusting, though, sort the clothes out. Some can go straight in to wash, and if there is a heap of socks and pants, and somewhat lively T-shirts, I recommend putting them straight into the machine and switching it on before you lose momentum.

I'm sure you have a pile of clean stuff, so put it away where it belongs. I pair socks and roll pants, then do that Marie Kondo folding for T-shirts (it's the wish version, I'm not that precious), but if you find it easier just tipping them into a drawer, then do that. Fold trousers and tops and hang shirts if you need to. Tailoring really does need hanging as it's laborious to iron. Anything dirty can go into a laundry hamper – as long as you will actually wash it, it's not a portal to another realm.

Now do the dusting and vacuuming. Put away your cleaning kit. Get into your pyjamas, clean your teeth, get a glass of water and clamber into your lovely bed. It's 6pm, a perfectly reasonable time to go to bed. Lay back on your pillow, spot another damn cobweb. Tomorrow is another day.

HALL AND STAIRS

I left this until last as not everyone has a hall, and depending on your lifestyle, it can be a dumping ground for shoes and bikes or a wasteland of unclaimed post.

Quick Fix

If you can lose most of the coats, great, if not, hang them neatly and tidy enough to give a clear path into the living room. Shove clutter on any hall table into a bowl or a drawer. Wipe dirty finger patches quickly with white spirit and polish with spray polish. Leave a lamp lit to make sure you don't trip, but turn the overhead light off.

Things You Might Not Have Tried

It is often quicker to use a dustpan and brush to sweep stairs than to use the vacuum. Wear rubber gloves to pull hair and dust free from the carpet. If you see a rubber-bristled hand brush for sale, grab it; they are perfect for stairs.

Use a mirror or two in order to throw light into a dingy hallway. Apart from enabling you to double check your hair on leaving, they can transform the space.

General Tips

DO NOT hang keys near the door – a small bowl by the kettle is far safer. I'm not actually sure if the fishing for keys thing is urban legend or not, but I wouldn't chance it.

Get a really good doormat, and make sure that as you walk in the door, both feet land on it. I actually think a nylon turtle mat job immediately inside the door and a coir mat that you stand on to close the door behind you is the best set up, as you shut the door while wiping your feet. I've never removed shoes – our houses have always been too cold to go in stocking feet, and slippers are a nightmare because the dog always steals them, or I forget and run out to the shed with them on. Again, it's simply what you are used to doing. All I have to say is that small Lego bricks have never frightened me . . .

Do go through coats and jackets every so often as they need washing or taking to the cleaners every once in a while, and if you really don't wear it, either donate it or get rid of it. Hang unseasonal coats elsewhere if they are in the way – those big vacuum bags with built-in hangers are perfect to reduce bulk. As a reward for such devotion to order, I frequently find odd bits of change.

If you can feel a cold draught coming through the letterbox, put a flap on it. You can buy them, but a piece of lino duct-taped securely above (so the duct tape acts as a hinge) will be better than nothing. We actually have a door curtain as our door sits right at the bottom of the stairs, and curtains are a prime example of second-hand being an awful lot cheaper than new. If you are really skint, try to buy an old single blanket or bedspread, you can tack it up so it completely covers the door, then fit a tie-back to hold it away from the door during the day when you are in and out. Once you are home and settled in, untie it to make sure it sits tightly.

Reels of foam insulation tape or draught excluder (available in different widths and thicknesses) are relatively cheap and easy to apply, and when stuck all around the door frame are a big help in preventing draughts. Stick them to the edge of the door frame that faces you when looking out of the door, then the door presses them in place when it closes. They can be quite cheap, but the glue used on them can also be cheap, so they may not always last that long.

For a Thorough Clean

Once the general mess has been dealt with, sweep the stairs down with a brush, then wipe and dust the banisters (once again, we work top to bottom). Open the front door and kick the mats out – brush them down or shake. Brush the door frame and wash or wipe the door, both inside and out.

Run a broom around at ceiling height to knock down any cobwebs. Vacuum the floor and then mop it. Once you have mopped and the floor is dry, you can put the doormats back and close the door.

Now polish any wood and mirrors, mainly to make it smell fresh and pleasant!! Admire your handiwork, just as the Amazon man rings the bell and the dog puts grubby paw prints all over things.

WASHING

MACHINE-WASHING

Quick Fix

Almost everything can be washed on a gentle wash cycle; if in doubt and you need a clean outfit, then a hand wash cycle will safely freshen things up. Hang on a hanger to dry.

Things You Might Not Have Tried

Using a spoonful of washing soda to prewash oily work clothes.

Use a large mugful of white vinegar to wash towels – it helps to remove soap residue.

General Tips

Washing with no additives works surprisingly well, and never be tempted to add loads of products – I promise you, it is not necessary. Using more than you need can make clothes smell slightly rancid and allow them to get dirty even faster than usual . . . If you want to smell nice, buy a designer cologne.

How To Wash Perfectly Every Time

Doing the washing does have some simple rules to follow. It's not some arcane art, but just a basic grasp of what you are actually doing. All machines differ in the programmes they offer, how they go about delivering results, and also, I have no way of knowing how old your machine is!

So, we come to fabrics. Natural fibres are either animal hair (wool, cashmere, angora) or plant fibres (cotton, linen, ramie). Synthetic fibres are plastic.

Animal Fibres

Animal fibres are excellent insulators but need careful washing. Wool remains an efficient insulator even when wet. Tweed is a preferred fabric for many in the country as it keeps you warm far better than many waterproof materials. When animal fibres absorb water the tiny scales on the surface stick out a bit, and if they get agitated, they start to mat together and then the fibre shortens and becomes felted (shrinking). This is permanent and it cannot be undone. Most modern washing machines offer a wash for these fibres or you can do it by hand. My preference is to use the machine, because getting the water out of hand-washed items enough so that the clothes dry in a timely manner can pull them out of shape far more than a spin cycle in your machine, which spins them more gently but fairly efficiently. You cannot tumble dry them as they will shrink. The only exception is if you want a seriously warm, waterproof garment for a toddler – boil a man's woollen jumper. It will be waterproof and warm but so thick and stiff (because it has shrunk considerably) the poor mite won't be able to move their arms.

93

Silk is the casing from silkworm pupae and it's both warm and cool. I would wash silk as for wool, although it is far less likely to shrink and really does need ironing, so it's best avoided if you are a bad ironer. It's a high-end option for thermal underwear, though, and I'd never iron that.

Plant Fibres

Cotton, linen, ramie and the like are fibres obtained from a plant. They are biodegradable and usually cool to wear. They absorb sweat from the skin and can be woven for light translucent weightlessness (lawn) or thick strength (denim). They take dye well and are long-lasting, and although they shrink on the first wash, most modern clothing is pre-shrunk, so unless it says otherwise you are fairly safe washing it. Because it absorbs water into the body of the fibres, it needs spinning fast to remove as much water as possible, but it can usually be ironed with a fairly hot iron.

Synthetic Fibres

There are a few which are neither synthetic nor natural (viscose being one), but for simplicity, I'll say that synthetic fibres are plastic fibres that are extruded very thin, spun into thread, then woven or knitted. The fibres do not absorb water and they don't shrink (although they can contract), but as plastic melts and softens with heat they are best washed on a cool cycle. For the same reason, they don't get spun so fast, because there is less water caught in them, but if you crease them heavily you cannot iron them at anything but a cool temperature in case you melt the fibres.

So, this is why your machine splits into two types of wash – synthetics at cooler temperatures and lower spin speeds, and cottons at higher temperatures and faster spin speeds. Wool is off on its own.

The way the machine treats these while washing differs, too. The cleaning is achieved by the drum rotating and the clothes tumbling and falling with the soapy water, then as they move, the fibres stretch and open to allow water to penetrate and dirt to fall out. Cottons cycles do this vigorously, the fibres themselves absorb both water and stains so it needs some proper movement to clean efficiently.

Synthetic cycles are more subdued, the fibres themselves do not absorb any dirt or water so it simply needs to dislodge what has got caught between them, therefore it spins more gently to avoid creasing the fabric.

Wool cycles just shake the drum gently, they increase the temperature slowly and spin firmly but at one (lower) speed to avoid that fatal locking of fibres.

Things To Wash With

I prefer to use an eco liquid detergent, as I rather like frogs and I hate the idea of my laundry detergent harming them, but many people prefer either pods/capsules or powder with a distinct smell. Then there are the additions, such as fabric conditioner, scent boosters, disinfectant, etc.

Pre-Treatment Spray

This is a must-have. It's a liquid mix of a detergent and oxygen bleach, which you spray on the marks and stains prior to putting stuff in the machine. For deodorant stains, you drench them in it, likewise with bloodstains. As it hits a mark you will see it fizz up, and for deep stains you can reapply several times. It's invaluable and saves rewashing so many things.

Enzyme Soaks. This is BioTex; although other brands may exist this is the only one I know of. It is basically the enzme stuff that is in biological Detergent. You can add it to non-bio detergent as the 'bio' element, or you can make up a solution and leave things to soak. It is designed to help with organic marks and works best at blood heat. It does not work in very hot water, and is ineffective in cold.

Detergent

This is the stuff that gets rid of dirt. Whether you choose liquid or powder detergent probably doesn't matter, but do read the packaging and put the recommended amount into your machine. If you have hard water, then add in a dessertspoonful of soda crystals and just dose the detergent as for soft water – usually about 35 ml, which is around a spoonful. If you put more in than is required, then it accumulates in the fibres of your clothes and gives a slightly grey tinge over time; it can also ruin your machine. The manufacturers go to great lengths to get it right, so start with their recommendations and adjust only slightly. If you prefer the tablets then use the correct number as indicated by the manufacturer. Make sure to place them towards the back of the drum though to avoid them lodging near the seal of the door.

Pods/Capsules

These are all-in-one washing detergent pods/capsules. You don't need pods/capsules AND powder/liquid AND conditioner. Just the pods/capsules.

Scent Booster

Genuinely, I've never used one of these, I think scent boosters are a gimmick – all they do is add smell. I wear perfume, and that cheap acrid smell clashes horribly with what I choose to wear. However, you do what suits you, but for all that is holy do NOT pour them into jars as a budget potpourri, or put candles in them as they are flammable.

Laundry Cleanser

This is disinfectant for clothes. If you wash at 60 degrees, it's not needed, in fact, most bacteria is removed by washing even at 20 degrees, so don't be panicked by advertising. I can see a possible use for them after illness, or for seriously smelly socks, but again, it's largely advertising hype. Fine if you can afford it but even then, I'm not a fan. The obsession with germicides strikes me as very unhealthy; cleanliness is one thing, but we need microbes for our health.

Fabric Conditioner

Fabric conditioner is a waxy liquid designed to coat fibres to keep them smooth and separate, it reduces static and can reduce wear fractionally. It also smells and uses animal fats, but vegan versions are available, plus unscented ones if you hunt around.

Don't use fabric conditioner on towels or cleaning cloths as it reduces absorbency, so instead of your towel getting you dry, it just shunts water around. It goes into the final rinse water, never with the detergent – detergent is formulated to remove wax and grease, so it will remove the conditioner from the water before it deals with the dirt in your clothes, meaning your clothes won't be properly cleaned and the conditioner will have been rendered useless and washed away.

Oxygen Bleaching Agents

Now these I am a fan of, although for many uses the doses given are nowhere near strong enough. You can buy a liquid version, too, which saves having to dissolve the powder. They are perfect for organic stains, like blood, to brighten and lighten, and they are the first line in stain removal. They are used prior to washing or after (if you inadvertently dyed your shirts pink during a wash, for example). But do wash as normal after using as they can leave a rough residue.

Colour Catchers

These are useful things, but don't overpay for them. The idea is that they absorb any free colour that comes out as you wash and prevent it from re-depositing into other clothes. Perfect for when washing clothes that are white with other colours. If you doubt the necessity of only ever washing pure white with pure white, I advise you to put a colour catcher in a mixed wash and see how it comes out.

Good Practice When Washing

For best results, do not overload the washing machine. As I have mentioned earlier, the fabric needs to tumble and fall freely in order to get clean, so if you stuff the machine to the top, the clothing or linen simply won't get properly cleaned. If you are on a budget, then turn the temperature down (heat is expensive, motion is less so). It's also worth pointing out that the machine will last far longer if you don't overload it, as the wear on the bearings, which turn the drum, is reduced.

Sort your washing before you start. Whites should only ever be washed with other whites in order for them to stay white. Wool is obviously done alone in a separate wash. Then it depends on how much you have. Personally, I sort by colour – dark blues, greens and blacks go together regardless of fabric, lighter shades of the same, then dark reds, browns, etc. Just try to wash like with like.

If you have a mountain of stuff, then sub-divide the colours into natural fibres and synthetics and use the correct programme for each.

I only use detergent once every three or four washes with towels (to avoid a build-up), and never use conditioners (a towel's main purpose is to soak up water, and conditioner hinders that).

Clean the filter at the bottom of your machine regularly to avoid blockages and unnecessary hassle. See page 103, 'Washing Machine Blockages' on how to do this. This section will also help you if you experience a problem or blockage in your washing machine.

White Bits on Dark Clothes

A question I frequently get asked is how to deal with the white flecks that seem to get deposited on dark clothing in the wash. The most common reason is that you have been using loo roll as a tissue, left a sheet in a pocket and washed. Loo roll is made to disintegrate in water and a single sheet will end up all over your clothes.

It is difficult to remove because the shreds are really fine and embed themselves deeply, so try to prevent it happening in the first place. Use tissues or kitchen paper where possible (though tissues can also cause a similar effect if left in a sleeve or pocket before washing). Train yourself to never put paper in a pocket. Most important of all is to go through every single pocket and crevice before you put something into the machine.

Once it's there though, you need to shake the dry garment out as hard as possible to dislodge any bits that come free (it's best to do this outside in the garden if you can and if you have outside space available). On woven fabric, it is worth using one of those velour napped clothes brushes. Then wash the clothes again, but try to put as little as possible back into the machine, as you want the tiny shreds of paper to come free from the clothes and be swept down the drain.

If it isn't loo roll, it will be something else that has disintegrated, so be a little wary when washing straight after as that stuff can linger in your machine. I usually wash light-coloured towels to try and pick up any bits. A light-coloured towel itself can lose bits though, so if any items are starting to look thin, be careful. At the opposite end of its life, new and high pile fabric can shed a lot for the first few washes, so do try to wash like with like as much as possible.

Washing Machine Blockages

When you open your washing machine after a cycle and it's either still sodden or full of water, do not panic, it happens a lot.

First, look at the bottom of your machine where you should see a circular plate that unscrews or unclips to reveal the filter. Now look to see if you have a drainage tube – it will be a small cap which, when unclipped (BUT NOT OPENED YET!!) and pulled firmly, is attached to the end of a rubber tube. Make sure you have pulled the tube out fully. I did a TikTok about this, didn't pull the tube out properly and flooded my lobby. With this in mind, before you start to try and clear the blockage, get a bowl that holds a gallon or so. Get a few old towels as well because water will get on the floor. It might be wise to have the mop and bucket to hand, too. If you are in a flat, perhaps setting up a wet and dry vacuum (if you have one) to suck up the water might be wise.

Now, hold the tube over the bowl and remove the cap. Hopefully water will come cascading out and into the bowl. Once the water has reduced to a trickle and then has stopped, recap the tube, empty the bowl (you may need to do this a few times, depending on how much water is still in your machine) and put a roasting tin surrounded with towels under the filter cap and remove it again. More water will come out. Wait until it stops. Deal with the water, then pull (unscrewing it first, if necessary) the entire filter free and clear of the machine and give it a good rinse to remove any debris from it. Put your hand into the hole and feel for the impeller. It's a fan contraption that spins to swoop the water up and out of the drain hose. It might have a hairgrip, cocktail stick, coin or something else wedged in. If your hands are too large, enlist a small but obedient child (turn the machine off first; social services take a dim view of injured children) and get them to check for debris.

Hopefully the blockage was obvious and is now clear. Put everything back together and run a rinse and spin cycle to finish the washing.

If there isn't a drain tube, then once the lock has disengaged, use a mug to bail out the water. Remove the sodden clothing and dump it in the sink. Once you've got as much water out as possible, you can open the filter cover. Be aware that a LOT of water will pour out in a hurry, far more than if you had a drain tube. Continue from that point, as above.

The alternative, if you are strong enough, is to pull the machine out and lower the main drain tube from the machine to empty it. The only slight issue with this is that when you push it back you must make sure you don't kink the tube.

If you have cleared the filter and it still won't drain, you may need a new pump. However, you may still be able to spin the clothing – the water won't leave the machine but the clothes will be a bit better.

Whatever you do, remove the clothes from the machine because if they sit in the machine, they will start to smell truly foul.

HAND-WASHING

Most modern machines have a very reliable gentle or hand wash cycle, and for most delicates this is more than adequate. You may see special detergent advertised for delicates (although I rarely bother to use it). It is a very neutral detergent that usually produces a little more foam than the standard stuff. The foam acts to buffer the garment while it is being washed.

There will be times though when a particularly fragile or precious garment needs attention. Seriously fragile antique stuff will need a conservator to assess it, and most museums will advise if you ring and ask. The V&A in London have a day once a month when you can take stuff in for them to look at. Well worth doing if you need advice.

But if it is merely a childhood blankie, or your grandmother's blouse, then a little care means you can do it at home . . .

Fold the fabric carefully, to fit into your bowl or sink. Fill the sink with warm water and add a little neutral detergent, then gently immerse the fabric and leave it to sit for 15 minutes. This gives the water a chance to soften any dirt, then pat the fabric gently all over to move it up and down in the solution without twisting or pulling the fabric. Depending on the amount of dirt that floats free you may want to repeat this step a few times. Then you repeat with clean water until you are certain every trace of detergent is removed. Drain the sink and gently lift the fabric up to allow it to drain into the sink for a few minutes. After it has drained for a while, place it on a clean towel and gently roll up the towel, then leave for 30 minutes. Unroll, and if necessary, repeat until the fabric no longer drips. Lay it flat over a rack to dry and then if you are confident, gently iron using a medium heat.

DRYING

Now, this is where what you need and what the tumble dryer delivers may differ. Like washing machines, tumble dryers vary in price and in what programmes they offer. There are vented, condenser and heat pump tumble dryers, so do some research and choose a machine to suit your needs.

If you are line-drying, you might cut the spin speed of the cotton cycle to avoid creases – the drying is free and it is far easier to iron if the fabric is uncreased. Likewise, using a tumble dryer costs quite a lot of money and the steam and heat produced helps remove creases, so even with synthetics you may prefer to spin at a higher speed, then remove the clothes from the tumble dryer while still warm and fold them neatly.

Never tumble dry animal hair. It will come out toddler-sized and cannot be stretched. Dry clean only.

Good Practice When Drying

Do make sure things can dry easily, because damp washing starts to smell musty fairly quickly. It's easier to do one wash every day and hang it out to dry with plenty of air circulation, than to try and process everything in one day, then struggle to dry it.

Try loading the washing machine at night and setting it to run, then hang out or up (inside on an airer or on hangers) in the morning. A good tip to dry an airing rack of stuff while you are at work is to position an ordinary cooling fan towards it; it keeps the damp air moving away quickly.

If you have a tumble dryer, then remember not to overload that either – it's far cheaper to do two 30-minute loads than one two-hour load. Remember, for safety, never leave a tumble dryer running overnight or when you go out. This absolutely is a fire risk!

Be vigilant to clear the filter(s) after every single load (and empty the water tank, if you have a condenser-dryer), and if it is venting into a hose and then to outside, you should clear the hose of lint at least once a year. Apart from the potential fire hazard, your dryer will be far more efficient if it's kept clean.

If your tumble dryer is a condenser dryer, it has both a water tank to collect the water from your clothes and a condenser, usually a series of metal fins that allow the steam to condense over them, so be sure to keep this as clean as possible – I generally rinse them out under the tap, but using a fine brush to get in between the fins can help with this. If your tumble dryer is one of the newer, more efficient (and more expensive) heat pump dryers, you should clean out the lower filter from time to time. Check the manual but it is usually found in the bottom corner of your dryer, in front of the heat exchanger.

Generally speaking, it's easier to just fold and put away washing as you get it dry. Those heaps of clean stuff waiting to be put away are so depressing, and if you brace yourself, you can tidy quite a lot away in 10 minutes. Then turn around and spot a single dirty sock behind the door . . .

Dry Cleaning

There are several reasons an item is labelled Dry Clean Only. Firstly, there is an element that cannot be immersed in water – this is often something like the stiffeners in tailoring which soften in water, causing the garment to lose its structure. This is common in very high-end bespoke tailoring. The cheap, ready-to-wear garments usually use iron-on polyester interfacing which can be wetted. In fact, the hospitality industry has spawned machine washable polyester suits for bar tenders and waiters. They can be washed and usually tumble-dried (and often don't need ironing).

The second reason is that while perfectly washable, the garment is incredibly difficult or impossible to iron, and washing distorts fabric, which usually means some degree of ironing is needed. Even if you can pull and stretch something back into shape, it may well need ironing to look halfway decent.

The third reason, which is very common, is simply that the manufacturer is aware that the garment is shoddily made and does not want to guarantee it in case it becomes unwearable when washed.

The last category just needs care. Viscose, for example, has no wet strength, it goes hard when wet but dries perfectly, so if you are unsure, then work out how much the garment is worth to you, whether you can iron it, and then wash on a gentle wash to see how you get on.

The first reason above is a really good one, and if you buy, inherit or otherwise acquire a bespoke item of tailoring, then don't wash it. Don't, for that matter, chuck it into the high street cleaners without making sure they have some understanding of what they are doing.

The other two reasons above are slightly less firm, so look closely at the garment and think about your ironing skills and the materials involved. It might be perfectly possible to put the garment on a gentle wash, then pull it into shape, dry on a hanger and then iron to perfection.

Steamers

Some steamers are strong enough to steam a garment into shape – most charity shops have steamers to both sanitise and smooth the garments, they rarely iron and I have yet to find one that washes, which is why they ask you to ensure all donations are clean. Sometimes, if they are feeling kind, they may accept a donation to steam a garment for you. Just be generous and don't make a habit of it.

Pilling

These are those little balls that cover the surface of fabric after a while. They are small tangles of fibres still hanging on by a thread. They are unsightly but easy enough to remove, although be warned it is a sign that the fabric is wearing. I shave them off with an old razor; you can buy purpose-made shavers, but I just find one that looks semi-reasonable from the bathroom and shave away. The other caveat here is that on knitted fabric it is possible to sever a whole thread, and if you do that you will cause a hole or run. Fix that as soon as you spot it, because a tight stitch or two can prevent a massive and unfixable hole from developing later in the day.

IRONING

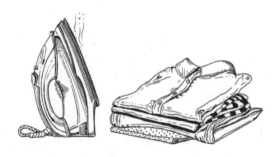

Those of you who watch my videos will have heard me explain that I am a terrible ironer. Most of my clients only ask me to iron flat things. But I'm not being entirely honest here, because I can iron perfectly well but not at speed, so the cost per shirt for me to iron is astronomical. I'm also not keen on doing it as I find it incredibly tedious. Some of my friends adore it and find it both relaxing and calming.

Those who can iron to perfection with a cheap iron have a rare skill, and if you want to look well groomed it is one you will appreciate learning. Even bargain basement clothes look good when pressed and presented nicely.

However you feel about the task, there is a correct way to do it in order to get a good result, so I will cover the basics and you can see how you get on.

Firstly, your iron. Virtually all modern irons are light-weight with a steam function. You fill the reservoir with water, which releases small amounts of water onto the hotplate, it then turns to steam, which shoots out of a series of small holes in the bottom of the iron. The com-bination of heat and moisture allows the fabric to be pressed completely smooth and flat. If you live in a hard water area I advise using deionised water (a few pounds per 5 litre from a hardware shop) in an expensive iron, or just use previously boiled water from your kettle if your iron isn't expensive and finicky. This saves having to descale the things, or having it spit crumbs of limescale over your little black dress when you need it in a hurry.

Your ironing board is usually a coffin-shaped flat board of metal or wood on legs, which allows it to be stored flat against a wall. The board is covered in fabric (sometimes padded) and

if that is worn or torn, a replacement can easily be purchased and fitted. You can iron on any flat surface instead,
but ALWAYS use a towel and never iron on your carpet.

Your iron will have a temperature dial showing three settings, cool, medium and hot. Your clothes will have a label
showing the recommended iron temperature, so follow
that as far as is practical.

In the machine-washing section earlier (see page 91), you
will remember I mentioned that most synthetic fibres
are plastic and so melt. Quite a lot of clothing is a mixture of synthetic and natural fibres, especially shirts.
Polycotton needs a cool iron as the polyester element
melts at a high temperature – if you run a hot iron over a
polycotton shirt, you will feel it sticking and see a burnt
mess on the soleplate of the iron. The cotton part may not
go flat at the lower iron heat, though, and this is where
a cotton pressing cloth comes in handy – it allows you
to use a hotter iron without melting the fabric. It won't
protect everything though, so be extremely careful with
light synthetics; if you melt a large hole in the fabric, you
have ruined it.

Cotton and linen can both take high heat and a lot of
steam, in fact, I suggest ironing both of these when
slightly damp, because when they are completely dry it

can be almost impossible to remove the creases. I also keep a spray bottle of water to hand as I find it easier to use than the spray function on the iron itself.

Start by pressing small cotton things, such as pillowcases, handkerchiefs and napkins. I know they aren't ubiquitous any more, but they will give you a feel for what you are doing. Do check to make certain they are cotton, not polycotton. If they are polycotton, then either turn the iron down or use a cotton pressing cloth, which is any sturdy piece of cotton or linen fabric, or a clean linen tea towel – or try both methods to find out which is easier.

If you iron pants and socks, you may be the offspring of a demon ironer. I'm absolutely certain that they can guide you through this far better than I ever could, so I shall assume you are only going to press the essentials.

Shirts

Start with the collar, taking care to flatten the points and smooth the neckband out. Move on to the yoke – that is the bit of cloth that sits on the shoulders – although not all shirts have this, so if not, it is still worth doing now in order to press the seam where the arms join the shoulder. In order to do this you hold the shirt sideways and put the shirt over the nose of the ironing board so that the arm itself hangs down to the floor. Do this to both sides.

Now move on to the cuffs, then the sleeves, making sure the seams are smooth and keeping any creases that are fixed into the cloth as single creases, as you iron. Tram-lines running up sleeves or most casual trousers are unsightly.

Finally, iron the two front sections and then the back. I prefer to hang shirts, but if you don't have the space, try to fold them as carefully as possible and don't overload the shelf or drawer. It is disheartening to carefully press a shirt only to have to repeat the whole process at 6am in order to get out the door in a smart enough condition for work.

Trousers

Casual trousers are rarely pressed with front seams today, a few sorts of chinos look nice with a crisp seam running from a pleat at the waistband down, but mostly they just get pressed smooth.

Tailored trousers do need pressing carefully – I suggest using a cotton cloth to avoid any hint of shininess. I start by turning them inside out to press the pockets smoothly, using the nose of the iron to get into the pleats at the waistband if there are any, and ensure the seams inside are flat. Turn them the right way round and press the seat and the front, then hold by the bottoms and line up the seams and any creases. Carefully press the legs to obtain a crisp crease down the front of the legs and a smooth front where the leg bends at the top of the thighs. Again, I prefer to hang tailorings to keep them looking crisp and smart.

T-Shirts and Knitted Cottons

Quite often when washed these distort, with the seams no longer running straight but twisting across the body. This is because they were not cut with the grain of the fabric running straight up and down. This is frequently done to get more garments out of a length of cloth, so it's a common fault, especially in very cheap garments. If you spot this when you hang them up to dry, you will realise why so many garments tell you to pull them back into shape while damp. So try to get the damn thing as straight as possible when you hang it to dry, and do the rest with the iron. It makes the clothes more comfortable and it looks better, so it is worth doing even if you don't normally iron T-shirts.

Knitwear

Knitwear can be ironed but is best just pulled to shape when wet; ironing can make it look flat and sad.

Structured Jackets and Coats

Structured jackets and coats are best dry cleaned, unless your ironing skills are on point. To get them looking sharp, you need things such as tailor's hams to shape the shoulders and arms. If you are desperate to try your skill, then watch the videos of those who create these garments, but do not trust a 'hack' you see online. Sometimes though, a small patch you have sponge-cleaned needs a careful touch with an iron to bring it back to smooth, so just go very carefully and try not to melt any of the fibres.

GENERAL STAIN REMOVAL

The issue with all marks and stains is the same, no matter what the problem is – you have to find something to remove the stain without damaging the thing the stain is on, and sometimes that's just not possible. A huge amount of stain removal is just about using your brain. If you know what solvent any particular mark needs, and how that affects the surface it's on, you can work out where to start!

Not everything is reversible though, which is why prevention matters so much. Organic stains do tend to fade with time and UV light. Synthetic ones are less likely to fade with time. One reason the Aniline dyes were so remarkable was that, not only did they have a wide range of vibrant deep colours, they were also stable compared to vegetable dyes.

In this section, I have included some common stains/ marks and the solvents to use on them to remove the stain/mark. Two methods are usually employed, depending on the surface.

On hard surfaces, use a cotton bud dipped in the chosen solvent and gently wipe a tiny patch of stain. If it's the correct solvent, the tip should have some of the stain transferred to it. Now look closely to see what damage it has done. For example, has it removed the varnish or paint, or has it eaten into the plastic? If everything looks okay, then proceed with caution, if not, then consider if the stain can be concealed, painted over perhaps, or can you just ignore or get used to it?

On fabric or carpets, we usually drip or lightly spray and blot. Treat the stain with a drip/light spray of stain remover, then blot with a towel or a white soft cotton cloth. If you can get a pad of towel or something underneath, all the better. That is obviously easy with a shirt or the curtains, but far harder with the living room carpet. Always proceed gently – it's easy to become too enthusiastic, then instead of a tiny red mark, you end up with a huge pink one.

Badly Tarnished Copper and Brass

Use brown sauce for this . . . honestly! Tomato ketchup works, but brown sauce is better. Paint it on thickly with a brush, leave it to sit for a bit, then wash it off. After that, you simply polish up with metal polish. As a side note, there are now metal polishes that you rinse off, and they do get rid of tarnish very easily, but I have noticed that the metal then tarnishes really very quickly afterwards. I suspect the traditional metal polish leaves a thin film of whatever petrochemical the manufacturers use, which provides a slight barrier to the air. If I use one, I always try to do a final polish with Brasso just to preserve my hard work for a few weeks longer.

Burn Marks

When you burn something you change it, and the burnt material cannot be restored. If the burn is not too deep, you can sometimes remove the burnt surface. Burnt carpet can have the browned tips to each fibre carefully cut away. This can leave a slight dent in the surface but very often that vanishes after a few weeks of foot traffic across it. Wood can be sanded back and refinished, although you have to be careful to blend it in.

Cat and Dog Pee

On almost anything, pee can linger. Obviously if you can immerse something to wash it then it does wash away, however, pets and children, as well as the ill, often pee on beds, carpets and chairs, which can prove a challenge. Try to avoid, and where possible put waterproof mattress covers on, and use washable incontinence pads on chairs and in places where pets try to pee.

There are a variety of enzyme-based shampoos to address this issue and they are remarkably effective, but they do need time to be allowed to do their job. I have found that spraying a solution onto the mark and covering it avoids re-contamination and gives the bacteria a chance to munch away and do their job. If your pet has repeatedly peed in the same area(s), then you must put something over the mark, as they have far more sensitive noses than humans and once they know a particular spot is safe to pee (I'm sure your living room rugs are notably free from wolves), they will continue to pee there. So put something waterproof, absorbent and preferably wash-able over the place once you have cleaned it to allow the scent to fade away. Obviously, a vacuum extraction machine is the most effective cleaning method after the solution has worked, but if not, just sponge clean. Cats spraying outside calls for a bucket of hot soapy water and a deck scrub.

Candle Wax

BEFORE you iron it out, freeze it – simply place a bag of frozen veg on top, then scratch and crumble as much hard wax out as possible. Then and only then move on to using the iron, and, if possible, place a pad under, and a pad over. For preference, use an old towel or kitchen paper. The brown paper trick isn't quite as effective, as you are turning the solid wax into a liquid and need to absorb it as fast as possible, so use the most absorbent thing you have available.

Chrome

This is the hard, bright silver finish often found on bathroom accessories. It is attractive and easy to clean, simply needing a wipe with a soft cloth and possibly a

HOW TO CLEAN EVERYTHING

polish to make it sparkle. Its benefit is supposedly that it does not rust. The chromed finish itself doesn't rust, but with age and a damp atmosphere, you will see small rust spots breaking through the finish. You cannot restore the chrome as this is effectively a small hole. However, if you use a paste scourer to remove as much of the rusting as possible, it becomes less obvious. You can spray a clear lacquer over it, but that will only slow things down a little. However, once the process has started, it can take several years before it looks so unsightly as to need replacing.

Deodorant/Antiperspirant and Grass Stains

I include an entire section here as I get asked daily about these stains. When people talk about deodorant, they usually mean antiperspirant, which often contains aluminium salts. May I suggest switching to a deodorant instead. Sweat is a perfectly normal human response to heat and stress and only becomes a problem if you smell unpleasant to others. Antiperspirant can stain clothing and can be remarkably difficult to remove, whereas a deodorant will prevent the odour but is less likely to damage clothing. A lot of our bodily fluids are mildly acidic, and can, over time, bleach colour. Women's knickers often bleach over time and this is perfectly normal.

The reason I lump deodorant/antiperspirant and grass stains together is that they get forced into the fibres of your clothes. The reason they can be the devil to shift is that once embedded, they are deeply engrained, so need care and attention to ensure the cleaning fluid actually reaches the stain.

Pre-treatment spray (applied to the garment before it is washed in the machine – see page 96) – and lots of it – will work. Spray, spray again, drench the stain in it, then rub the mark with a nailbrush and give it at least 10 minutes before you start the washing machine. Make absolutely certain you do not overload the machine, and give the machine a longer wash.

Mud

Mud contains not just organic stuff, like earth and grass, but bits of grit and sand, too, which get lodged into sports kits and trousers, and often the two come hand in hand. It can be difficult to remove. The organic parts come away with pre-treatment spray (see page 96), but the fine grit will not dissolve in anything as it gets driven deep into the fibres and cannot simply be bleached out (it is, very literally, a microscopic rock), so it can persist. Try not to worry about sports kits – despite what detergent adverts like you to believe, many rugby shirts are stained beyond redemption long before they develop a hole.

The only thing that removes the mud is to allow it enough time in the wash to dislodge itself and fall free. The material needs to tumble and fall in water so most of it can work its way back out. Allow 24 hours' soaking time in something like Biotex to get the process going, then, taking care not to overload the machine, give it a long wash. Heat won't help much here, so keep your electricity bill happy by turning the temperature down to 30 degrees, but allow a long cottons wash.

Other Quick Fixes

Biro: try methylated spirit to remove it.

Crayon: use isopropyl alcohol.

Dirty Fingerprints on Wooden Doors and Rails: use white spirit on a rag for these.

Lily Pollen and Turmeric: use oxygen bleach and/or sunlight.

Lipstick and Grease Marks: these are always difficult (it's the little red mark versus the large pink stain situation), so try using a little cornflour to soak up as much as possible, then once you've got the bulk up/off, use an oxygen bleach to gently remove the rest.

Permanent Marker: use isopropyl alcohol or acetone (try to use these as they are; nail polish remover, for example, contains so little acetone it may not work).

Powdered Make-up: gently work in a little cornflour to pick up the stain, vacuum up, then use an oxygen bleach stain remover to remove the rest.

Red Wine: use oxygen bleach (Vanish or peroxide).

Sticker Residue: use lighter fluid or WD40 (but first, try gently warming the sticker, it may just peel off). I am also informed that the Avon Skin So Soft Oil works (this is the stuff that also repels biting insects).

Tar: use eucalyptus oil.

MOULD

This is another thing that crops up frequently. Mould is a form of fungi and the bit you can see is the fruiting part. The mycelium, which is the actual body, is hidden under the surface. Mould spores are extremely prevalent in the air, and listening to a Fry and Rutherford podcast, I learned that we breathe in an average of eight spores with every breath we take. All fungi need moisture and mould usually crops up due to damp, poorly ventilated conditions in the house. Always try to find out the source of damp when you find a mould growing.

There are a range of household mould treatments for the less serious patches you will find around the place. Borax works well, but is not for sale in the EU, and the most common ones contain either benzalkonium chloride or sodium hypochlorite (aka bleach). The latter will take the colour out of the black staining from mould, but also from your clothing and anything else it touches.

Dry Rot Fungus

The most unpleasant one to contract is the dry rot fungus, which can ruin your house and be really costly to treat. The first sign can be what appears to be a mushroom growing from a skirting board, then further investigation reveals the stringy mycelium eating into the frame of your house. This absolutely needs professional attention, so do not muck about, call in expert help immediately.

Black Mould

Bad black mould is dangerous but it isn't anthrax, and it's very common in bathrooms. You can clean the stuff off (although it does stain), but unless you address the cause, it will keep coming back. Remember the actual mycelium is under the surface and your mould killer may not penetrate deeply enough to catch all of it. Hence why either curing the damp or increasing ventilation is needed. Often people stand in the shower, gaze up and notice a black patch above them on the ceiling and then panic. The other really common place is in the silicone and grouting behind the taps on the sink and around the bath and shower.

To remove it, spray with a mild bleach solution and wipe. When it looks clean, spray some more bleach solution on and leave to dry. Do be aware that the black mould can stain and be virtually impossible to remove completely from silicone and grouting, but before you even think of replacing them, you must address the ventilation.

Use the vents in the bathroom, open the window, and if your window frames have trickle vents in them, ensure they are clean and open. Leave the bathroom door open when you're not in there, and if you have a shower curtain, open it or flip it over the rail once it's dry to allow air to circulate. If you have a generally damp house or flat, you may benefit from a dehumidifier in general. While small amounts of mould aren't worth getting upset about, a damp, mouldy environment is really not at all healthy and needs addressing as it can lead to breathing issues. If you manage to sort the problem out and decide to repaint, I strongly advise using stain block before painting.

In winter, a single-glazed window will get condensation on it. While you can take steps to minimise it by reducing the damp in the house, warm moisture-laden air will dump that moisture on any cold surface it touches. It's worth wiping the frames dry (keep a few old rags to use for this) and then when you draw the curtains, just mop up any water. Later in the book, I explain how to upkeep wooden frames, because the moisture will lift paintwork and putty and, over time, the frame will rot out. I loathe cleaning deteriorated frames. Halfway through you have a nasty lumpy black mess of paint flakes, crumbs of putty and black mould – not appetising, and because of that it takes a long time. Hence why I think it's worth putting another chunk of time in to fix them up a bit, as it saves an unholy mess next winter.

BIG STUFF

Cleaning the bigger stuff can be daunting. However, there are a few things to remember that will help. Things which are wet are really heavy, really hard to manoeuvre and will drip a lot of water everywhere while you try to manhandle them, so before you start cleaning your rug in the bath, give some serious thought to what you will do after.

Things that are left damp start to smell quite quickly indoors. If you are able to, do you have a place outside – perhaps under a carport or similar – where it can dry? Please also remember that a warm damp rug or footstool will start to smell musty really quickly, so good ventilation is essential. In colder weather, it will be better to have something in an unheated garage or carport than inside with poor ventilation.

It may prove to be a sensible option to either buy or hire a vacuum extraction machine that comes with an upholstery nozzle that you can whizz over a three-piece suite and a footstool in a morning and have excellent results. If that is not possible, then try the following tips.

Rugs

For heavy stuff like a rug that you have immersed in your bath, I suggest using an A-frame of some description, which will support the item over the bath (it's a rug, it's always a bloody rug, or a weighted blanket), so the water can drain away. For it to drain freely, there should be a half-inch gap between the rug and the bath. It could take days to dry, so I suggest doing it in summer when you can leave the window open with a fan running over the item. It will be really heavy and hard to manoeuvre, and if it touches anything it will act as a large cleaning rag for the surface it touches. You can end up with a far dirtier rug than the one you started with!

The best method I have found is to put a rug over a fence and pressure-wash it. I've seen plenty of people suggest taking it to a garage and using their jet wash, but I refer you to my previous comment – it will be heavy, sodden and impossible to manoeuvre without dragging on the ground and picking up dirt. You could possibly take it home on a tarpaulin in a transit van, but it won't be easy.

Weighted Blankets

Weighted blankets dry faster. The beads that provide the weight are usually glass so they don't absorb water, which means they don't gain as much water weight when washed. I would never risk them in a machine though as a small tear or hole could dump a large quantity of beads into the guts of your appliance and the repair bill would be astronomical!

Mattresses and Footstools

Mattresses and footstools need turning sideways so the surface is vertical rather than horizontal. This is simply so any water will not penetrate into the depths to then turn funky in a week. Ideally, this is a job for a hot summer's day. Raise the item up off the ground so water can drain away, shampoo the surface with a sponge and rinse down. If you can do this early and keep the item in the sun for the whole day it is possible to have the item back in use fairly quickly. I suggest blotting the surface as dry as possible to avoid watermarks, then return to the correct orientation to dry.

Large Duvets and Quilts

If you have a mark or spill on a bulky item that will not fit in the washing machine, you have two choices. You can take it to the launderette or the cleaners and get the entire thing cleaned. If it is slightly grubby all over then this is your best option.

Or, if you simply have a stain on it, then you can wash just the stain. I bunch up the marked area and use an elastic band or a piece of string to make a lump, which I can wash and rinse in the sink while the bulk sits on the worktop. Before you untie it, squeeze the now-clean lump with a dry towel and put it outside to dry. It is a kind of spot-cleaning extra and is really useful when sponging isn't quite enough. You may need to iron the patch thus cleaned afterwards, though, as it will be quite creased.

Sofas and Chairs

Again, these are items best done outside in good weather, but if you are only spot-cleaning marks you need to take care not to end up with a watermark. This is caused when water drifts outwards, taking colour and dirt with it, then it evaporates, leaving a ring. The way to avoid this is simply to dry out as much free liquid as possible by blotting it firmly with a dry pad or cloth, then gently rubbing to get the surface as dry-looking as possible.

Coats and Jackets

Wool tailored coats are not suitable for washing at home. They often distort slightly when wet, and the padding and stiffening inside bunches up, making them impossible to iron. Check tailored coats in general, as some are fairly easy and come out well when washed – my daughter's Primark ones get washed twice a year. Others simply crumple out of shape.

The rainproof jackets are treated with something to repel water and usually have washing instructions on them. Generally, they need washing on a cool wash with a very short spin. Down jackets and Parkas are much the same, but due to the greater thickness, they need a longer faster spin.

If your garment is a rain jacket, it will need reproofing after washing and drying. I like the wash-in stuff, but be aware that you may need to apply heat to activate it. I found that a hair dryer works if you haven't got a tumble dryer.

Down jackets really should be tumble-dried to get their poofiness back. If you haven't got a dryer, then hang them to dry, and every 30 minutes or so take them down and shake them as hard as you can. The same thing applies here as it does with everything else, it needs to dry quickly enough that it does not smell musty.

Pillows

Most pillows are washable, but as with any other large item, it is the drying that proves to be a hurdle. The exception to this is the cheap polyester pillows. They are made of cheap polyester wadding, rolled and flattened, so when you wash them, it starts to come unrolled, and instead of a bouncy rectangle of filling, you have a weird trapezoid lump. Some cheap blown fillings also tend to clump and go lumpy. It is often the case that the more expensive pillows wash better.

If you do ruin your pillow, it is often possible to unpick one end, refluff and organise the filling inside, then re-stitch the case.

Whenever you have new, or freshly cleaned pillows, always put an undercover on them. I'm tempted to say put two on, a mite proof one first, then a slightly thicker, padded one. If you do that, you will not need to wash the pillows much at all, if ever.

But if you have pillows, and they need washing, let's see how . . .

First things first, do you have a tumble dryer? If not, I strongly recommend you do not wash your pillows until summer, simply because if you cannot dry them completely within about 36 hours, they will smell. I also suggest it might be unwise to wash foam pillows at all, unless you can put them in full sun for a day or two. Sleeping on slightly mouldy pillows is really unhealthy.

Now, having said that, most pillows wash well. You must balance the washing machine drum, i.e. have two pillows, one either side of the drum, so that the weight will not try to tip the machine over. You can absolutely spanner the machine if you don't. I suggest using either a wool wash or a synthetic cycle as these won't move the pillows around too much, and this reduces the chances of the filling shifting around and going lumpy. Then set the spin as fast as you can.

Now, it's highly likely that the machine will refuse to spin them at first because they will be too heavy. You can take them out and squeeze out as much water as you can, or just leave them in and put them on a spin-only cycle. If you listen, you will hear the machine start to spin, then it never picks up speed as much as it should. However, every time it does that it removes more water, and there- fore more weight, and after a few tries, the load will be light enough to spin at full speed. Once it finally spins at speed, give it at least one more full spin, simply to get as much water out as you can.

Then dry the pillows. If it's warm and sunny, you can hang lighter pillows up to dry; feather and down ones benefit from a firm shake every so often during drying to restore the bulk. I prefer to hang them up for an hour or so, then tumble-dry them for a while, then hang them up for a bit more.

You may find the surface gets a bit hot in the tumble dryer, so take them out, bash them about a bit and leave to cool. The middle may still be damp, so give them a chance to steam a bit (in the sun), then put them back in the dryer again. Once they are looking really plump, if you bury your nose in them, you can usually feel and smell if they are still damp or if they are bone dry.

Feather-, down- and blown-filled pillows are pretty straightforward to wash. Foam ones need a little more care to ensure they are properly dry, but as long as you pay attention, the results are good. If the middle is not dried within about 48 hours, they will start to develop mould and are unsafe to sleep on. So, if you do not have a tumble dryer you need to put some thought into drying them, in full summer sun for two days they may be okay, but unless you are certain do not risk it.

Soft Toys

Many of our soft toys have just gone into the washing machine over the years, but a toy containing sawdust or cardboard should be assessed by an expert prior to cleaning, as they could be rather more precious and fragile than you expect. Ignoring the properly old toys, many of us have an elderly companion who needs a refresh. If it is not valuable or especially fragile, a childhood friend may need to be taken apart, cleaned and re-stuffed. Too much love can take it out of a bear, you know.

There are quite a few videos on YouTube of this, but the procedure is fairly straightforward. You unpick a fairly central seam on the toy and remove the stuffing, the 'skin' is washed as outlined before for fragile fabric (see page 106), then dried. Any minor repairs can be done once dry, then the toy is carefully re-stuffed with new stuffing and sewn up.

Rucksacks and Cases

I actually wash most of our smaller daypacks/rucksacks in the washing machine. A couple have cardboard stiffeners, which stops me doing anything but spot cleaning, but otherwise, I just do up all the zips and clips, then wash on a quick cycle. It freshens them up nicely and if you have spilt a drink inside, it is the easiest way to clean them. If you can't wash them, then sponge down carefully and leave hung up to dry.

For suitcases, I just wipe them down carefully. Hard shell ones might benefit from a little Cif to remove marks on the outside.

Sheepskin

I wash my sheepskin boots (the Ugg type) on a wool wash in the washing machine, then put boot trees in so they dry nicely. You can also wash sheepskin rugs – just make sure you shake them firmly every hour or so while they are drying to stop them going stiff. DO NOT tumble dry either, because even if the skin will take it, the glue that holds the boot soles in place will disintegrate. Don't overdo the detergent either.

Leather and Suede

Leather usually requires a leather cream or saddle soap; saddle soap is mostly for full-grain leather and can darken it somewhat. Leather cream is an emulsion of oil and water, so it will dissolve both kinds of stain. Most coloured leather is actually a plastic coating on top of

145

leather and can be wiped with a damp cloth. Scratches and cuts cannot be removed, but you can buy renovating pastes that re-colour the scratch and make it less obvious.

Suede is more delicate. You can buy suede shampoo, but do follow the instructions carefully as you don't want to create a watermark. Suede rubbers and brushes work by brushing out any loose dirt and then removing a small amount of top suede to reveal a clean underneath. I suggest you always treat suede with a Scotchgard treatment before use. It's an invisible layer that repels water and dirt and is well worth paying a little extra for.

Wax Clothing

Here is another one for arguments. The makers of waxed jackets usually say to just brush down and sponge them clean. For the most part, that is all they need, but just like sheepskin (see above), you can wash them. However, if you wash them on a long, hot wash, you will certainly remove all the dirt, but also the protective wax and you cannot replace that completely. So, wash them on a cool wash instead. This won't remove the wax, it may look a bit cloudy, and ingrained dirt won't come out either, but it does a good job of freshening up the garment. I use liquid soap, but there are also specialist washes sold for this. The lining comes up nicely, too, if that smells a bit stale and sweaty, and being cleaner it makes small repairs (like replacing a zip if it's worn) much easier.

Wash the wax clothing on a cool wash with a slow spin, then put on a hanger(s) to dry, pulling each garment into shape as you do so. Once dry, have a look over and do any small repairs.

Now, to re-wax. I have a tin of Barbour wax, admittedly it is thirty years old, but even when new it was difficult to use and has a distinctive smell. I don't mind the smell at all, but in a crowded London Tube train it certainly makes its presence known, so it's not for everyone.

I also have a different tub of garment wax, which is far easier to apply and has no smell at all. My jackets always need the shoulders re-waxing and I also go over the seams carefully. Have a good look and any patches that look pale should be waxed. After this you iron it – the heat helps the wax to soak into the cotton and the whole thing looks great. BUT never try this without using a thick ironing cloth, otherwise the melted wax will ruin your iron. Use a medium temperature and keep the iron moving. The other option is to use a hair dryer, which evens out the wax and usually smoothes the fabric nicely, too. A genuine Barbour jacket can be sent back for repair and a re-wax, but there is a fairly hefty price attached. I'm also informed that the results can be rather variable. Once done, hang the jacket to air out before wearing.

Agas

I've put this here rather than in the kitchen section. Agas are expensive to buy and expensive to run, but those of you lucky enough to have one will want to keep it in good condition for as long as possible.

Solid fuel Agas are rare now. Gas seems to be the most common, but many country houses are not on mains gas and instead rely on oil. While they are a heat retention cooker and designed to be on all of the time, you can turn them off completely for maintenance. If you just turn it down to pilot only, the top between the two plates will still be too hot to clean properly. So, once a year, book the service and turn it off completely. Make sure you have paste scourer, caustic oven cleaner (paste or gel), cloths, wire wool and a few Brillo pads and a pair of rubber gloves. A small caddy steamer (see page 35) is handy as well.

Leave overnight to cool down, then open the doors and lift off, but remember where each door hangs as they are essential to maintaining the heat zones. Open the lids and begin. Firstly, wash the doors. Most marks will come off with a paste/gel oven cleaner, but caustic oven foam will get rid of any stubborn ones. Polish each door with a cloth and lay it out to dry; water will dribble out as the doors are hollow stuffed with insulation for at least two of the ovens. I never bother doing anything other than vacuuming out the insides of the ovens themselves, as they are mostly self-cleaning.

Cover the area between the two plates with a thick layer of caustic oven cleaner, as well as any other patches of burnt-on stuff you can see. The Aga definitely needs to be cold to do this, because if the pilot is on you will simply create nasty fumes and even more dried gunk. Methylene chloride paint stripper used to be the go-to stuff for cleaning this off, but it has been removed from sale due to health concerns. Other paint strippers don't work nearly as well, so just buy the strongest caustic paste/gel you can get. Now, using the paste scourer and possibly a brillo pad for stubborn marks, clean the front – this is usually rather grubby behind the hinge posts and there are often splashes down the front, so use a toothbrush to clean the thermometer and the badge.

Now come back and look at how much the caustic paste/ gel has eaten into the burnt-on gunk. Sometimes it needs to stay on for several hours, but once it looks done, then start to wipe it away, using wire wool to help dislodge it. The caddy steamer is perfect for jetting out inside the plate lid hinges – they do not come off and it's surprising how much dirt and grease comes away.

Use paste scourer on the chrome lids and on the aluminium underneath as well. If you really want to you can use metal polish to shine the aluminium to a proper sparkle, but I don't as it is not an economic use of my time. If you DO decide to do this, remember those lids get super-hot, so get every trace of polish off. Once you start, you have to continue until it is all done – there is no leaving it half done.

Once everything is clean and polished, you can re-hang the doors. Given how central to the kitchen an Aga is, it really does pay to look after it.

Open Fires and Wood Burners

I live in the south of England and we mostly use wood as a solid fuel. It was strange going up to Durham a few years ago to find that coal fires were still in use. The smell is entirely different, and coal spits embers out far more than wood, so all the pubs had really singed rugs in front of the fires. No matter how you fuel your fire, get a spark guard, especially if you have an open fire. A spark guard is a screen covered in fine metal mesh to stop any flying embers spitting out of your fire and setting your carpet (or something nearby) alight. If you have children, you also need a proper child-safe fire guard and you must ALWAYS have it secured in front of the fire.

New regulations are going to be coming in to regulate emissions from domestic fires. The use of coal fires in England up until the 1950s caused buildings to be covered in a thick layer of black soot, leading to one of several clean air acts passed in Parliament. Most buildings have now been cleaned, but there is occasional evidence of the heavy pollution in cities. The famous Pea Soup fogs, which appear in novels, do still occur but not in Britain. They were deadly as they crept inside houses and rendered entire cities blind. There is a necessity for limiting what we can put into the air as climate change is destabilising our weather worldwide, so anything and everything we can do to mitigate this has got to be good.

However, domestic fires still exist, and if you have never had an open fire or wood burner before it might pay to know a few rules.

Before you start a fire, the fireplace or wood burner must be emptied of ash from the previous fire. Be aware that due to the insulating properties of ash, red-hot embers can lurk, hidden away in the heaps of ash you are about to clear out. Use a metal bucket and shovel, then when the fire is clear of debris, move the bucket outside. Only risk transferring it to a plastic bin or bag (or the compost heap, if you have one) if it is completely cold all the way through – melted bins/bags are not uncommon. Have to hand a few sheets of paper (newspaper is traditional, but as print media is less common I find the paper packing inside Amazon parcels ideal), a firelighter or two (the natural ones – often little bundles of wax-coated wood wool – are great), a little kindling (small bits of dry wood

and twigs) and a few small dry bits of your main fuel, be that coal or logs.

Scrunch up your paper and lay it on the grate or floor of the wood burner or open fire, put your firelighter(s) on top, then make a little wigwam of dry kindling on top. Over that, lay a few small dry bits of your main fuel. Heat rises and flames need fresh air, too, so build a loose structure vertically. Put a match to it and wait. Your kindling should catch light fairly quickly, so put a bit more on if your fire looks a bit sparse. You are trying to get a nice hot but small fire burning away, then you can slowly introduce a bit more of your main fuel to get a slightly larger but slightly slower fire. Once you are happy all is going well, close the door of your wood burner or make sure a spark guard goes up in front of an open fire.

Until you are familiar with your fire, avoid going out and leaving a roaring fire going – I usually knock ours flat before I go out, so it does not suddenly start burning hard. Make sure your chimney is swept every year (some house insurers require this as standard practice) – chimney fires can go unnoticed for several hours and are often extinguished by the fire department sticking a hose down your chimney and pumping gallons of water down. The mess is unbelievable, and your belongings will be ruined.

Windows and Glass

All sorts of tricks and tips get floated around, of which a clean microfibre cloth and some window spray is the most effective way for a quick polish. However, the best results of all are gained by actually washing your windows. You are trying to remove a very thin greasy film that builds up and smears. It can be really hard to spot, you think the surface is sparkling, then 2 hours later with low angled light it becomes apparent it's not.

Use hot water with a few drops of washing up liquid in, then properly wash each window, just as you would a plate, round and round in little circles over every inch, then use the squeegee to remove the water and a bit of soft cotton rag to mop up what has pooled at the bottom. I actually have a window vacuum and it does work, but the only thing it saves me doing is mopping up the water, so it's an expense you probably don't want or need.

GENERAL MAINTENANCE AND REPAIRS

General Maintenance

If you rent, much of this will be your landlord's respon-sibility, but I have found that shabby cheap houses often have landlords who don't object to you decorating as you please, but who also fail completely at doing basic maintenance – which offsets the cheap rent a bit, but keeping the place in good order marks you as a desirable tenant and also makes your life a bit nicer. However, things like roofs and gutters really are down to them, so if there seems to be a leak, or a blocked gutter, then email or ring your landlord and/or agent to notify them. I also suggest that if you are renting a flat, you ask the landlord to appoint a plumber to do any water-related work, and make sure you have an out-of-hours contact for an emergency. Water can cause serious damage and you do not want to be liable for water damage to the flat below.

Now, to windows. If they are single-glazed and in painted wood frames, check the condition of the paint and the putty holding in the glass. The best time for this is during the warm weather, when you can scrub the frames with a mixture of mild detergent and hot water, replace and repair the putty (putty is fairly cheap to buy), then lightly sand and repaint to seal the putty in. I have found if you do this every year there is rarely any need to do much more work, it keeps the mould at bay during the winter and generally makes the place look smarter.

Look up at the gutters as they will need clearing of debris at least once a year. However, I suggest you pay someone to do this unless you are confident at heights, as a fall from guttering height can be life-changing.

Look up at the roof after any storms to check if any slates or tiles have been damaged; you absolutely need your roof to be water tight.

Walk around the outside of your property to check for anything out of the ordinary, like cracked brickwork perhaps, or pointing between bricks looking worn and in poor condition.

Dripping taps are easy to cure early on, so don't wait until the drip becomes a torrent. Bleed your radiators once a year as soon as you turn the heating on for winter.

All of these things are demonstrated on YouTube far better than I can explain, so do go and watch. If you are a home owner, it is in your best interests to keep your home as well maintained as possible. If, God forbid, you are forced to sell, then the sale price will be far higher if it is well decorated and in good condition.

General Repairs

It's worth knowing how to do simple repairs, to both your clothes and other things in general. Mending holes in socks and jumpers doesn't require much skill and can save an awful lot of money in quite a short space of time. Again, this is not something I could cover easily in writing, but YouTube has millions of instructional videos. Just a word of warning though, don't just copy the first one you see, watch several and delve into the comment section, as I have seen several videos which are completely inadvisable.

Changing fuses in plugs is easy, resetting your trip switches is easy, but do leave more risky electrics to the professionals.

Decorating

Preparation is very important here. Use dustsheets, wrap furniture tightly, cover shelves and put carpet protector down. Plaster dust will work its way into everything, it is damaging to fabric and paper, and it is the very devil to vacuum away. The reason professional decorators get such nice results is due to the preparation they do in advance.

Walls and woodwork are washed and sanded back to smooth, and imperfections are filled and sanded. Light switches and sockets are unscrewed so paint can go slightly under where they sit, yet will not mark the surface. Check your skirting boards – a day spent sanding the top edge where it meets the wall at 90 degrees will save you 2 days trying to cut in a neat edge. Sand all existing woodwork down to both provide a slightly rough surface and to smooth blemishes flat. Please do this because it is absolutely why some rooms look spectacular and other very similar ones just look tired.

Wash your walls with Sugar Soap (see page 22). Start at the top and work in horizontal strips from side to side. Any tarry stains, watermarks and dark bits will benefit from a coat of stain block to prevent them from slowly migrating to the freshly painted surface. Stain block is usually a shellac with white pigment, but I have in a pinch used the colourless shellac furniture polish.

Buy good-quality brushes and clean them scrupulously after every job. You can tightly wrap a brush or roller – in either a plastic bag or cling film – to keep for a day if you still have work to do, but make sure it is completely paint-free at the end of a job.

The most valuable tip I can give you is to never be too fashionable. Carpets, large items of furniture and dark paint colours are really hard to get rid of, yet a cursory glance on the internet will show you how badly many deeply popular styles have aged. Try and get either something so very full of itself it will never be either in style nor out of style (if you are not entirely sure, emerald green velvet with pink trim will bring out the colour in your eyes), or buy a fairly classic, neutral thing. My own preference is for cream sofas, which I then cover with lots of vet bedding as my dog, Hollie, is black.

Grey is on trend, but if your entire house is charcoal-grey paint, you will find it is virtually impossible to paint over – dark painted walls are better off being covered with lining paper prior to the new paint going on. It will be a bit of a faff applying the paper, but far less work than covering the wall with three layers of paint. Perhaps choose a lighter grey that can be painted cream more easily? But if you do need to paint a navy blue wall with magnolia paint, it will also be cheaper and easier to just use lining paper to cover up the deep-coloured paint.

Look at the trends you like and assess how well they will fit with your lifestyle. Mirror tables and toddlers are not a match made in heaven. By the time the toddler is old enough to be reliably not sticky, they will be horribly dated and scruffy. Your house should give you pleasure, but remember it's YOUR house, it's not there to impress the neighbours.

Very often a room can be updated by simply changing light shades, cushions and the smaller accessories, giving a nod to the current trend but not going full-on.

Health and Safety

It seems a permanent whinge among some older people when they complain that health and safety is ridiculous, that the world has gone mad (and on ad infinitum until your teeth jangle), but the guidance was put out for a reason. People have died, and still die, from stupid preventable accidents. Wear safety goggles, have someone hold your ladder, read the instructions and file them away, and be careful when using sharp implements or electrical bits of kit.

If you have children or pets, then keep dangerous things under lock and key. Never underestimate the climbing abilities of a toddler as they are perfectly capable of reaching the top of most worktops, and cupboards and shelves are merely a challenge, especially if they suspect sweets are involved. I speak from experience here; none of mine were harmed, but I have spent time in A&E worrying furiously.

If you do suspect your child (or your pet) has eaten something dangerous, then go to A&E (or the vets) at once.

The faster they get there the easier the treatment; if they can rinse the stuff out of the stomach quickly enough, you can usually avert much harm.

Pests

I'm reluctant to recommend annihilation for uninvited guests. Sometimes it is the only way to handle the issue, but you can make your home less inviting. Pesticides in the home are safer than those outside. I spray for moths, confident that I am not going to poison other animals further up the food chain. I am less certain in the garden.

Clothes Moths and Carpet Beetles

Never put clothes away in a drawer or cupboard when they are not clean, and make sure you open drawers out and organise and shake the contents on a regular basis. Vacuum wool carpets regularly, especially under things, in corners and behind heavy curtains. If you spot the slightest sign of anything eating your clothes (or carpets), then you need to spray. I use a basic permethrin spray, as it (allegedly) does not persist in the environment. I also use mothballs for clothes; the traditional really smelly ones work but that smell persists and clashes horribly with Guerlain. I favour the Zero In range because it's effective with little smell.

Fleas mean your pet(s) need to be treated. You can get either tablets or spot-on flea treatments from your vet or you can buy a vet-recommended household spray. Fleas lay eggs that stay viable for a remarkable length of time, but the various treatments, including the household spray, last several months and kill the little buggers as they hatch.

Mice and Rats

Firstly, you need to remove any source of food, then you need to work out where they are getting in and block the holes. Walk around the outside of your property looking for small holes (this isn't always so easy with an older property though, as there tend to be lots of small nooks and crannies!), remembering that rodents only need a tiny crack to get through, then block the hole. If you are certain this is the entry point, then fill the hole and put mesh over it. If not, just block it up with some paper and come back in a few days to see if the paper has been moved. Look closely around baseboards and in the back of cupboards inside, too; a popular entrance is through vents and around pipe work. On a rainy day, little mouse prints can often be seen (or they'll leave droppings behind). If you act quickly and decisively, you may avert a proper infestation. If you don't nip it in the bud quickly, I'm afraid you need to steel yourself and use poison. I hate it, and I've been known to get up at 3am to retrieve the bait in case I commit rat genocide. Rodents, especially rats, breed incredibly quickly and they do carry disease. They can also cause an awful lot of structural damage, so while I am happy for them to live nearby, I cannot allow them to live in my house. The sonic repellents seem very effective but you really need to ensure you have the entire footprint of your house covered. It may also be worth considering getting professional help if you do have an escalating problem.

Glue traps/boards are vile, evil and downright wicked and often cause things to die a slow and painful death – the traps only work if the animal enters the trap straight on. Poison is relatively painless, but you must use it carefully following the instructions and be vigilant to remove any corpses in case they become food for anything else. Sadly, there is no easy answer. I have a live trap as we do get the occasional rat wandering in through an open door, but our dog quickly alerts us to an intruder and a little chicken or chocolate usually entices them into the trap. I have no illusions, if I release them into a field over the road they will be back in the garden before dawn. As long as they stay in the garden, I am happy.

RENTING AND GENERAL HOME THINGS

Renting a Property

First things first, this is mostly for England. I have only ever lived and rented in England, so what I say here may not apply to where you live; I include it because the majority of my followers are based in the UK. Some advice is universal, but it is vital you are aware of your rights as a tenant, no matter where in the world you live.

When you walk into your very first place, be it a room in a 'house in multiple occupation' (HMO) or a large house, please realise you have both rights and responsibilities. I am absolutely not a legal expert, so please read all the bumph you can find, check those of your local government website and any local authorities that influence your area. Obviously, a lot of the information here is for renters, but owners have legal responsibilities, too, especially if you have a mortgage. If your mortgage is greater than your deposit, then in reality your bank owns your house and you are merely responsible for it. Be informed. If you are unsure, then ask – and not just the bloke next door or some random people on Facebook – people who are in a position to be accurate, which is often your mortgage provider or your agent.

Always get three quotes (not estimates, quotes) for any work that needs doing and check carefully into the tradesman's references. Go and look, or speak to people who have had work done. A friend recently spent hours emptying a kitchen late one night to facilitate the plasterer she was expecting at 8am the next day. He didn't turn up, and then vanished from Facebook. Luckily all she had done was expend time, but it could easily have been money.

Inventory

Before you move anything into your new place, you need to look at something usually referred to as either an inventory or a schedule of condition – it lists everything in the place and its condition and it is VITAL you check this over carefully. Any marks, scuffs or imperfections not listed need to be noted down, plus take a clear photo of each one as evidence. This information then needs to be emailed to the agent, because when you leave, they will take any damages out of your deposit, so having dated photos means they cannot claim that the badger-sized hole in the bathroom door was done by you, likewise, the huge mark on the carpet that was hidden by the bed.

In England and Wales (I'm unsure of Scotland, due to a different legal system), your deposit MUST, by law, be held in a government-approved scheme, so you can dispute any charges your landlord may try to enforce. Evidence from dated emails and photos will weigh heavily in your favour. Once you have done that, you can move your stuff in – unless you want to clean first – and get settled.

Household Bills

You may have bills included in the rent, but if not, you will most likely have to pay for your electricity, gas (if you are connected to the supply), oil or Calor Gas (if that's your source of fuel), water and council tax. If you have never paid these bills before, you might be wise to get a pre-payment meter for both electricity and gas. It can work out a little more expensive (do shop around as it doesn't have to be), but it saves you suddenly getting a very large bill you cannot pay.

And remember, you must set aside money for other bills. Your water is probably metered (so turn the tap off while brushing your teeth, etc . . . to save some money) and the bills come around every three or six months. I believe in Scotland it is billed in with your council tax, so if you do not know for sure, it is important to ask. It's worth asking about how much these bills are likely to be when you view the place. Sometimes cheap flats are so badly insulated that you spend so much on heating it would have been cheaper to stay in a hotel. If possible, ask the incumbent tenant – they often have salutary tales to tell. Heat is an expensive thing to produce, motion is less costly, so you can look at your appliances and they will tell you how much power they use.

Electricity is sold in kWh (kilowatt-hour), which is one kilowatt of electricity for one hour. Your electricity bill will tell you how much that costs, then multiply that by the number of kWhs you have used to give you the amount of your bill. For example, old-fashioned incandescent light bulbs were often 100W, so if you left that bulb switched on for 10 hours, it would use 1kWh of electricity.

Gas is sold by volume, as is oil, and is far harder to calculate as the amount isn't readily stamped on the things that use them, which always involve heat, so before you go nuts with your heating, do try to get an idea of what it will cost you.

You MUST pay your council tax bill; in theory, you can go to prison for non-payment, although that's a last resort. Most councils split the bill up into monthly payments; I actually pay mine weekly and make absolutely sure I keep up-to-date with it. There are various apps and accounts designed to help you budget, and you will save yourself a lot of misery if you learn to manage your money.

General Tips for Rental and Home-owners

Find out where to turn off the water – it's probably a stopcock (a kind of tap) under the sink – and make sure it actually turns. I recently got stuck at a client's house when a radiator sprang a fast leak while I was there. I could neither isolate the radiator nor turn the stopcock and the bowl was filling too fast for me to leave, which meant I had to either wait for their return or flood the bathroom and very probably the flat below. Water causes a lot of damage very quickly, so knowing how to limit that is important. Once you have turned off the water, you may have to turn on taps and turn off the water heater – I'm sure you all saw those poor people in Texas when a sudden cold snap caused their pipes to burst.

Learn where the gas turns off, where the fuse box for the electric is and how to reset fuses. Take a picture of both the gas and the electricity meters (and oil/Calor Gas tank gauges, if applicable) before you set foot inside, so you can make sure you aren't paying for someone else's power. You will need a special key for this in order to open the box. It's usually a triangular one. They can be purchased for a few pounds. I have one I keep in a drawer that does a variety of types.

If you plug in something and the lights go out or the router goes off, unplug that item before you try to reset the fuse – it's probably faulty. It's also often the iron.

Also learn how to reset your boiler, and how to adjust any heating and hot water timers. No one wants the heating to come on as you leave for work, but have it icy-cold when you get up. I'm not including instructions for this, as the variations are massive, but if the manual is not in the house, look it up on a search engine, then either print it out, or write it down and keep it to hand. The manufacturer and model number of your boiler will usually be on the front and that should enable you to find the manual.

Have a torch that you can easily put your hands on; if it's a wind-up one you will not need to check it has batteries as often. If the lights go out, you may not have your phone to hand.

Find out what day the rubbish is collected, and where you should put it. Some councils have quite a complicated but efficient recycling system, others don't. Put an alarm in your phone so you don't forget.

Put important documents (passport, driving licence, insurance details, etc) together in a file and store them somewhere you can grab them in a hurry if you need to. In case of fire or flood, it's handy to be able to find them and it's expensive and time-consuming to replace these if disaster occurs.

Make sure you have a fire blanket in the kitchen. I also have a small fire extinguisher by the sink. If you set fire to your toaster, it might come in handy, but DO NOT take risks – fire spreads fast and burns really hurt. It's better you survive unscathed, than you collapse saving your second-best wheel of cheese. Small extinguishers are only for preventing a very small fire from turning into a big one, not for fighting a true house fire.

Test smoke alarms and carbon monoxide (CO) alarms regularly – they save lives every day. Your landlord has a legal responsibility to make sure these are installed, too, but it is up to you to test them. NEVER EVER take the batteries out of smoke alarms to use in the remote for the telly. Families have died because of that. In case of fire, grab living things and leave. Phone the fire brigade and wait outside.

Fire moves much faster and is much louder than you expect. If the opportunity is there, close as many doors as possible, as depriving the fire of fuel and air may slow it slightly.

If you are trapped inside, shut yourself in a room, block the door gaps to slow the smoke entering, and stay low as smoke rises and fills a room from the top down. In case you need to exit through a locked and double-glazed unit, do not try to smash it with a chair. Sometimes you can pull the rubber gasket that holds the glazing unit in the frame and the whole thing will come free. If not, find something small and hard, a nail or screwdriver, and put it onto the window in a corner. Hit it as hard as you can with something like a hammer or a shoe. Where a chair will bounce off the glazing unit without damage, a sharp object hitting the corner stands a good chance of cracking the unit open. Beware of the glass; there's no point escaping a burning building only to die from blood loss instead.

If you live in a flat, consider your escape route should the stairs be blocked. If you are only on the first or second floor, you could ask your landlord to provide an emergency ladder.

If you notice water dripping from the ceiling, quickly check it's not something like an overflowing sink or bath (one of my clients had a fish tank that sprang a leak), then put a bucket under the drip and use something like a screwdriver to push a hole where the water is dripping, to allow it to drain away easily rather than bringing the ceiling down. If you are in a flat, race upstairs and bang on their door, if there's no answer, call your landlord's agent or the building supervisor. If you are in a house, then turn off the water under the sink or wherever it is and turn on taps if you have a water tank in the loft. Then either try to find the leak, or call a plumber or your rental agent.

If you are in a rental, it is highly likely it is painted in either magnolia or white emulsion paint of the cheapest grade known to mankind. If you go to wipe off a mark and the paint comes off, do not fear. Large tubs of this paint are about £30 at a builder's merchant, so keep the place clean and if the paint looks a bit thin, it is easy to just repaint as you leave. Just check to see if you have a matt or silk/satin finish. It's going to be matt emulsion most of the time because silk/satin emulsion paint is easier to wipe and tends to adhere to the wall better.

Winter Chill

A lifetime of dealing with poor housing means I can make some suggestions. They come with a warning though – always have a CO alarm, check it weekly and be vigilant, as poorly burning appliances can easily make you ill, or kill you, and it's why landlords have a legal obligation to keep all gas appliances in good order. Many bad landlords have simply removed entire heating systems rather than pay for yearly checks. A shabby flat or house with no heating system, in an area with gas mains running in the street, may very well mean the landlord is a less than stellar example of the breed – do your checks before you sign the agreement.

Insulation and Draught Excluders

Sealing a home against draughts can cause gas appliances to burn badly, so that's why you MUST keep your CO alarm working; it can also increase the damp. So while I talk about sealing windows, etc, you must keep an eye out for black mould (see page 133). I've already banged the drum about dehumidifiers, and I know they are an expense many of you cannot afford, so other than suggesting they are a very worthwhile appliance for the renter, I will say no more.

Lack of insulation is the biggest reason you will be cold, so if you can put some cheap insulation in place, it is worth doing. There are grants available; if you do the research, your landlord may be willing to do the grant-funded work. Schemes change all the time though so make sure you are reading current information.

Single-glazed windows leak heat, so thick curtains are a must. Charity shops sometimes have them – ours has a deal with the dry cleaner's opposite and any abandoned curtains are sent over the road to be sold. It's surprising how often people take curtains off to be cleaned and never collect them. You ideally want thermally-lined ones; I bought our large door curtain cheaply from eBay, then lined it with bump (a cheap, thick lining to be found easily online) and it was quite easy to do.

Put strips of foam insulation tape or draft excluder around your door frames and any windows you cannot seal (see page 88 for more information on this).

Temporary double-glazing kits can be bought. They involve a cellophane sheet that you attach to the window frame with double-sided tape, then you use a hair dryer to shrink the cellophane tightly. They work very well, just be sure to take the tape off in the summer because if it dries on for years, you'll need to sand it off. An alternative is to use drawing pins or a stapler to tack bubble wrap over the windows. Just be careful your neighbours don't think you have a grow house in there. Having your door forced open at 6am is not a lot of fun, and it's quite difficult to claim compensation for any damage incurred. This is not, in fact, a humorous comment. I know someone who tacked space blankets up at his windows and was raided a month later. The lack of loft insulation and the shiny windows had led people to assume he was growing cannabis. Once the police have caused a large amount of damage, they are keen to find the very smallest piece of evidence of wrongdoing, simply to stop you claiming compensation.

Keeping Warm Inside

Electric throws and blankets for the bed are low wattage, so are cheap to run – they keep you toasty warm, but let the house get cold. Do not go to sleep with an electric blanket switched on because most of the time you will just wake up too hot, but it is also unsafe, and although exceedingly rare, there have been cases of heat stroke. We lower our body temperature naturally as we sleep deeply, and while getting into a warm bed is lovely, it may interfere with our sleep pattern if we artificially warm ourselves while asleep.

If you have pets, please tend to them, too. Hamsters go into hibernation if it is cold, so check if an immobile small animal is not moving, and for the love of heaven do not assume the worst! Keep your dog in a dog coat, and make sure all animals have a warm bed they can sleep in. Dogs run slightly hotter than people, so sleeping with a dog in the bed is a lovely way to keep your feet warm. Hollie curls up on my feet, then wakes me in the early hours as she is cold, then climbs in under the duvet with me.

It is cheaper to warm you rather than the entire room, so wear thermal underwear, gilets (you can get USB-powered heated ones), thick socks and slippers. Hats help, as do mittens. We have tried those over-sized hoodies and con confirm they are excellent for winter garb.

Please keep an eye on elderly or vulnerable neighbours, too. Be aware if post starts being left in their letterbox. In icy weather a frail person may be unsafe to leave the house to buy food. Don't be condescending, not all elderly people are sweet and lovely. A snide and nosy woman will stay snide and nosy but that doesn't make them less needy. Many extremely frail people have brains that work perfectly well, it's just their body isn't taking orders any more, and sometimes they resent or avoid asking for help. They still need it, so trade your help for their advice or knowledge. Being lonely is truly awful, so remember that if someone talks your ear off at the bus stop, it may be the first conversation they have had for weeks. It doesn't take much, a friendly word here and there, a chat over a cup of tea. Treat them like the people they are, not like a relic you are earning brownie points on.

Eat warm food, a bowl of porridge for breakfast, and toast plus eggs if you can manage it, and enjoy lots of warm drinks and soup. Now is not the time to try and eat salad, you need carbs and fats. Try to keep moving, too. If your day job involves sitting still in an overheated office you will really feel the chill when you get home, so get moving for a bit. Take the dog out, go for a run, then come in and huddle under a heated throw with a bowl of hot soup, before you slide into a pre-warmed bed.

For cheap calorific meals look at some of the wartime ration meals. I struggle to comprehend that as a major world economy I should be saying this, but here we are. It's quite stodgy but actually pretty healthy. Remember, too, that at that point in time central heating was extremely uncommon.

I find I manage quite well until we get to 5 degrees or less. Your own internal thermostat might differ, but I keep an eye on the met forecasts and try to pre-empt things by having supplies ready in advance. This year's trick was to prop some foil insulation up between my bed and the cold outside wall I sleep against. It's made an enormous difference.

EMPLOYING A CLEANER

If you decide your life needs a cleaner, it can be a little hard to know the do's and don'ts. I always suggest you ask around your friends and neighbours to find a few reliable suggestions. But do speak to a few people first. The most efficient cleaner on the planet is no use if he/she refuses to take care of the antique furniture. Or is terrified of your cat. You may also find that recommendations coming from those who see the world in a similar fashion to yourself will suit you better. It's not always the case, of course, but if you try to ensure that all your house is natural and biodegradable, it can be upsetting to then find bleach sloshed around everywhere.

If you decide to go the agency route, then be aware that you will probably pay a considerable amount more, you will not always get the same person or team, but the agency will take care of holiday cover and any problems you have. They are usually covered against accidents and sometimes the staff are CRB checked, too (if that is a concern), but obviously you get who they send, and some request that pets are kept locked away while they visit.

Be clear about what you expect to be done and make sure you have allowed them enough time. I had one woman insist that she and her daughter cleaned a four-bedroom house to perfection in 2 hours. Her perfection wasn't the same as mine and I am confident that 4 hours did not involve making beds and cleaning both the oven and the windows. Be reasonable about what can be achieved in the time you are paying for, and indeed if it is possible. Some furniture is too heavy to move more than occasionally; cleaning the oven can take an hour or more.

When you see a potential cleaner, walk them around your house and explain what you want them to do. If you only require what used to be referred to as the 'heavy work', i.e. vacuuming, scrubbing floors, etc, then make that clear. Warn them of any hazards, such as fragile curtains or a delicate and treasured Persian rug. Tell them what you care about, be it dust or cleaning behind the sofa. We aren't mind readers and don't want to spend our time cleaning skirting boards, only to find it's the lampshades you notice. We probably will do both, but not necessarily every week unless it bothers you.

Pay properly and make sure the terms are clearly understood. Some clients work, but as long as I appear at some point on my set day, they are happy, while others need me to be there exactly when I say I will. Be aware that a cleaner will have other jobs to do and you cannot just demand they stay longer or swap days; sometimes they will be happy to, but it might involve a bit of notice. One of my clients is elderly and struggles with rapidly changing plans, so for both our sanity I never stray from his scheduled slot. Make sure the cleaner knows where to find the mugs and tea bags, and access to the biscuit barrel is usually appreciated. Don't be condescending. Don't be rude. You are not better than your cleaner. Do not shout or yell in someone's face, be they the cleaner or someone else. If you treat me as your personal slave and assume I am stupid just because I clean your loo, the last thing I do on my last day before I leave forever is to clean your loo with your toothbrush!

Ask about the cleaner's flexibility, and ask if they usually take time off for a holiday. If so, are you prepared to pay them for that? Being generous usually ensures good service and loyalty.

If the cleaner is not doing something you require them to, then tell them and double check they have enough time. In nearly 20 years of cleaning, I have broken about two or three things, not due to carelessness as such but merely a second of distraction. If something is irreplaceable, then warn in advance that special care must be taken.

If you are convinced someone is honest, then give them a key, although I would suggest you establish where they live (just in case) and make sure that is written down somewhere. If you are not in, then make sure you leave a note with any special requests where it is immediately visible. I cannot count the times I have gone into a bedroom last to discover I am expected to strip and remake the bed linen, then wash and hang the stuff I have stripped.

If you ARE in when the cleaner comes, then settle down in one place while they work and ask them to chuck you out when they are ready to clean that area. While they deal with that, put the kettle on, make two mugs of tea and open the biscuit barrel. It's infuriating being followed around while you clean and it makes it quite difficult to work as well. The exception to this is for the large jobs that you need help with, but again, be clear about the help you need.

CLEANING AS A PROFESSION

I'm often asked about starting a cleaning business. I trade in England and I know the situation regarding tax and accounting varies wildly depending on where you live, so once again, please check all relevant requirements for your region. I must stress here that I am a self-employed sole trader. That is the one-person option, so you must register with HMRC and once a year fill in a tax return, as you are responsible for your own tax and National Insurance (NI). It sounds complicated but it really isn't, you simply need to keep good records of your hours worked/invoices and save receipts, etc. The government website will give you a clear guide on what to do; I have always found HMRC incredibly helpful and obliging when I contact them for help.

Some principles apply however you work. Be reliable, for example. If you say you will be there at 9am, then be there at 9am. If you are genuinely ill, then of course you cannot work, but waking up and not feeling in the mood is no reason not to go. Cleaning is physical work and really exhausting for the first few months, but it gets easier. Make sure you eat properly as you'll need the energy, and over time you will find yourself becoming remarkably fit. Look after your hands, wear gloves and use cream – those fingers are the main tools of your trade. You will find heavy make-up and false nails not terribly compatible with the job – make-up will run and sweat off; nails can break (and a torn nail can be excruciating). My nails now stay a shade over the tip of my finger and every time they get longer, I live to regret it.

Look after your back, too! This is really important.

I always have small dog treats in my pocket, simply so that any housemate with teeth regards me as an unalloyed good thing even if I do associate with the vacuum cleaner, but ALWAYS ask the client first as some dogs have medical issues.

Agency Work

This involves you being an employee of a company, so they are responsible for paying you and they calculate your tax and NI. This may mean you rarely go to the same place twice. You need to be a team player and pull your weight regarding what tasks you are asked to perform.

Depending on the nature of the agency, you can do anything from 3am office cleaning to a standard day-time domestic clean. If you cannot drive, you will be taken from job to job with another member of staff. This absolutely suits many people; night owls enjoy the dark expanse of offices and teams can form close bonds. If you are in a team and see things that concern you (and it is the nature of the job that sometimes you do), there is another person to discuss things with. It can be really tough at times to know if a person should be reported in order to access help, or if you are betraying a trust should you do so.

You usually have guaranteed hours and a regular pay packet, and usually accrue both holiday allowance and get sick pay. Depending on where you live, you may get a small amount over the minimum wage. However, just as landlords are not always honest and fair, so it can be with agencies, so please ensure you keep timesheets and your own records. You have rights in law, so please make sure you understand them.

Janitorial

This is slightly more encompassing than simply cleaning, as it usually entails being responsible for maintenance and minor repairs. You may be appointed as a sole caretaker or as part of a team with a specific building or complex in your charge. You may be asked to use some fairly industrial-looking machinery, such as large, heavy floor polishers, and be required to keep up-to-date with various industry certificates. If not, it may be worth asking if your employer will fund you taking the course(s), as they are inexpensive. Even if you don't keep up-to-date with them, it is useful to know what they entail and will help you work both safely and efficiently. The COSHH (Control of Substances Hazardous to Health) course is an important one for obvious reasons. Obviously in a janitorial setting, you will be handling and storing far greater quantities of the more industrial cleaning products than in a domestic setting. The general principles still apply though, industrial products may be stronger and lack the scent and colour used in domestic (supermarket) products, but the active ingredients will be very similar if not identical.

Manual lifting and handling is another course you may find useful, as well as the kitchen/food safety and hygiene and first aid courses. All of them cover the basic safety requirements you will need, and being familiar with them will be useful, especially if you move around jobs.

Domestic Cleaning

This is what I do – I am a self-employed sole trader/ worker. I enter clients' homes and (due to the fact I don't drive) use the equipment and supplies provided. This works quite well as my clients' needs vary quite con- siderably. Some absolutely prefer the simple eco-max approach and are happy to sacrifice glowing whites in order to look after newts, whereas others require glowing scented perfection achieved with an arsenal of products sold for one specific purpose. I must confess I find the latter rather trying, as it's depressing to clean an already clean home. I love the challenge of restoring an untidy and dusty room to a magazine photo shoot finish.

What matters in this case, more than anything else, is communication. If a client enjoys dusting and wiping the window ledges, they may only require you for heavy work, like cleaning floors, vacuuming and bed-making. So if you leave the floors dusty while you polish the windows, they may feel annoyed. The only way to deal with this is to ask – they can leave a note mentioning areas that require attention, or put you on a strict regime of floors only.

I once got fired from a job after one session. I went to a very elderly and infirm lady who had a truly ancient poodle. The place was absolutely filthy, yet she apparently had a woman come in to clean once a week. I scrubbed furiously and got it far cleaner, but a very long way from spotless. It turned out that she preferred the previous lady, who really didn't clean much, but just sat and drank tea. Apparently I was too bossy and she didn't really want a clean home but some congenial company for a few hours instead. I made her too aware of her own failing faculties. Some people just won't like you, won't want you in their homes, and no matter how efficient you are, there is no point taking offence at what comes down to a personality clash.

If the client simply requires you to keep their house clean, you need to engage your brain and your eyes. Some jobs, such as skirting boards and windows, may only need doing every month or so, but the loos usually need a clean every time you go. Every house differs, so it may take you a month or so to get into the rhythm of that particular household, plus often the demands change with the seasons. I am rural; I dream of a winter without mud and leaves, leaves and more leaves.

Find out how your clients judge clean. Some smell polish and floor cleaner and remark how nice it all looks, when all you did was mop up the spilled flash inside a cupboard. They need to be able to smell where you have been. Others like to see a sparkle shine, so remember to polish a tap and leave the work surface gleaming. One elderly and bedbound lady I had the pleasure of working for enjoyed hearing me bustle around; despite the fact she would never see the results of my labour, she liked to listen to what I was doing. She was perfectly capable of tracking me around the house though and could work out easily what I was doing; her hearing was truly excellent. Never assume anyone is a fool or unaware. I assure you that very few employers will let you take the piss for long. We all have off days, but make a habit of shoddy work and they will replace you.

Sometimes you will need to contact family or social services. Vulnerable clients may manage well in their homes with basic support, but may deteriorate and be in need of more care than you can ethically provide. Eccentricity can slide into dementia quite slowly, or it can happen overnight. Sometimes the answer is simple. Urine infections in the elderly can be spectacular, yet a week of antibiotics and a bit of monitoring returns them to normal. Safeguarding is an issue, and anyone who works in a client's home has a duty to look after their welfare. Equally, you do not have to take any abuse.

Quick Tips

Look carefully at each room, remember what you did the previous few weeks and do what needs doing. Remember to pull furniture away from the wall to dust behind; even if this only needs doing every month or so, it does need doing.

Move chairs and sofas, lift and plump up the cushions, and vacuum underneath both the cushions and the sofa itself.

Use a damp cloth-covered finger to run into the join between the carpet and skirting board when you wipe it down. If floors are solid, I simply run the mop over the skirting while mopping the floor.

Don't forget to wipe picture frames and check for cobwebs when the lights are turned on; every spring I am amazed by the cobwebs. I routinely run a vacuum around the cornice and inside and around the lightshade, but a HUGE cloud of previously invisible web always seems to show up with the spring equinox.

Try not to just rearrange the dust, do it with a damp cloth and vacuum as I explained earlier (see pages 75 and 76).

A lot of your job will involve saving yourself work next week.

You will learn an awful lot about your clients, but do NOT gossip. It will get back to them and you will develop a reputation as untrustworthy. You are in a position of trust. Some clients will treat you like 'The Help', so I suggest you find another job with someone who values you properly. Decent employees pay you properly, talk to you respectfully and let you make tea or coffee as required.

Pay Rates

When you quote your hourly rate or your price for a job, there is a formula. Assume you charge that rate for everything you do that is job-related, then remove the tax and the NI contributions, add in the costs you incur doing that job and see if you earn enough to live on. Charging £5 an hour will ensure you get more work than you can manage, but you won't be able to pay your rent and eat as well, in fact, you may find you are paying someone somewhere in order to work at all. The minimum wage is the absolute minimum you should charge, but I strongly suggest you pitch a few pounds over at the very least. You have travel and unpaid hours of work doing your books, as well as the paid hours, so factor those in. I virtually never take time off, and self-employed people do not get sick pay or holiday pay. If you expect an annual holiday, then factor that in, too. While employees do pay tax and NI, the employer also pays a share, and of course, THEY do the paperwork.

Agencies charge far more. Usually they pay their employees a shade over the minimum wage, but obviously they have overheads and office staff, so aim for a mid-price, enough to buy your loyalty but less than the agencies will charge.

Dealing with Extreme Mess

I am not going into serious hoarding clean up, that is a specialist job involving skips, shovels and hazmat suits. It is dangerous and not a job for an amateur. Like post mortem and crime scene clean up, you need good training. It is an area that can give great job satisfaction, and if you have the stomach for it, I suggest you find a company who is willing to take you on and train you.

I'm talking about the elderly and infirm relatives level of mess here. It is quite common, and as people's physical abilities decline, they are less able or willing to tidy and clean. This may be the time they decide they need a cleaner, often specifically in order to remain in their home. It is not uncommon for people to visit elderly parents as usual and notice a marked decline in a few months, then this rapidly turns into a mess which looks hazardous. The person may be really fierce and reject all help because they are not aware in the same way, and to admit your own decline is really, really difficult.

Be sensible. As long as they seem to be eating properly, look healthy and aren't in danger of falling down the stairs, they may be okay. Try not to fuss, offer grounded solutions and see how they are received.

One client of mine had taken great pains to future-proof her bungalow, getting a walk-in bath, adapting the kitchen and ensuring safety aids were in place. What she had not bargained on was dementia, which robbed her of the insight required to assess her situation. You cannot force someone to accept help. If you are working for someone elderly, it pays to make sure you have a point of contact for family or friends should you become concerned.

Tips to Help Elderly and Infirm Relatives and Clients

What you can do is, in advance, arrange for power of attorney (in England you can register with the office of the public guardian) that can come into effect should you need to take over financial affairs. The rules surrounding this area are quite robust, and rightly so, given the potential for abuse. It's easier to talk to someone before they need it so they can help set things up in a manner they are happy with. Always try to anticipate the future, you won't manage to do that most of the time, but every action matters.

Try to get important documents in one place, possibly lodging them with a solicitor for safekeeping. Go through photos together, write down who, what and where on the back. Record family tales, make notes on heirlooms and generally talk. If someone is frightened by their decline, talking about the past may help. It can be a way to strengthen a fraught relationship.

Going through stuff together will be far less stressful than trying to empty a house for sale in a few weeks. Link it to memories, make it a bonding exercise as far as possible and don't be afraid to lower bin bags of rubbish out of a window for later collection. You don't need to infantilise someone, but occasionally a little subterfuge to keep them safe is called for. That is said from experience. I defrosted a freezer for one client and discovered an entire drawer of salmon dating from the early nineties. She solidly refused to get rid of it. Totally unaware frozen food went out of date and convinced she would eat it at some point, she insisted I carefully repacked it. Then I waited until she was out of sight, bagged it securely, and knowing she would check the dustbin in case I had thrown it out, I lowered it over the fence to her neighbour. He was a star and knew to put it in his bin. Of course, she never went to use it and could have killed herself had she tried.

The following assumes the occupant will no longer be living in the house, but if they are, you simply ensure they have all the belongings that matter. If they are around, be mindful of the emotional distress this may cause, so perhaps sort one room a week to give them a chance to relax into the cleaner and clearer space. Don't steam-roller over all their requests either; very often you need to leave some of their stuff there, perhaps packed into vacuum storage bags and neatly labelled. This works very well with things they don't want to get rid of, but are unlikely to use. It keeps them securely sorted away from harm. Sadly, it also means that with an elderly parent you are simply sorting for later disposal. It can make your life easier later on. I can assure you that it is heart-breaking going through old shoes and dusty jewellery while grieving the owner. The sad moth-eaten hats that sat upon the shining head of your mother while she rocked your tears away are enough to utterly break you. Better to get them out of the way while she can still hug you back.

Rubbish. All cleaning starts in the same place – getting rid of rubbish. This is why I suggest you try to isolate import-ant documents. It is time-consuming going through huge piles of old magazines to find a bank statement or a solicitor's letter. Once rubbish is dealt with, then you can sort food-related things, washing up, clearing the pantry, packing china for donation or disposal, etc. Then sort clothing. Wash and put usable things aside, then put the rest to rubbish. If it is clean, then by all means sell it by the kilo for recycling, but this takes time you may not have.

With furniture, offer safe and usable stuff either to charities for sale (their standards are high though, so it has to be immaculate) or offer it free on a local buy and sell group.

Once the place is clear of all clutter, then you can start cleaning. Start at the top in each room and work down, cleaning the floor in each room last of all.

CONCLUSION

I have been extraordinarily lucky. While I rarely take a holiday or a break, I have found a set of clients whom I like, I enjoy taking care of their houses and I feel valued. I live in a relatively wealthy part of the country and my clientele reflect that. In an odd way, it has made me realise that money only solves money-related problems. Some things are made far worse by wealth, and most people who actually have money had a firm foot on the rungs of the ladder before they started to accumulate more wealth.

They eat and never worry about keeping a roof over their heads, but illness, addictions and other problems stalk their lives as much as they do with the very poor – they just suffer in comfort. But very often it takes one chance, one unlucky throw of the dice to change all of that.

I am a believer in a social democracy for just this reason. I'm not a fan of capitalism, but I am not an economist so am unable to see how a dominant system could be changed. I bow to minds greater than mine for that. But taxes should be used to give everyone a seat at the table and to make opportunity available to all. You cannot pursue a bright new future if all your waking hours are spent grinding away to pay the rent. Working until nearly 70, with a body that is worn out from hard graft in all weathers, is the only choice for many in the UK. We have paid taxes and National Insurance and have turned up come rain or shine. The only future is one of scrimping on cheap baked beans and a small and chilly flat with paper-thin walls. I failed with my children because I had to earn money, so they missed out on the trips and experiences their peers enjoyed. I don't think they mind now, and they knew they were loved and fed, but at the time they did mind.

I know from first-hand experience how lives can go wrong through chance rather than through choice. Try to remember that no one wakes up and decides to die cold and alone on the streets. Every decision they made was the best available to them at the time, very often they simply lacked education and choices. We have had a number of excellent and insightful books from people born into dire circumstances, and understanding how this translates into real-world outcomes is essential for us to have a fair and equitable society. Humans are a social species, so can we all please work to ensure our society works for all of us, meets the needs of everyone in it, and understand that until all our needs are met, the wants of others should wait. We have enough to provide for us all.

Acknowledgements

For Anna Steadman and the team at Headline, your skills are invaluable. For my clients who have availed themselves of my services over many years – thank you for the experience and lessons learned. Not a word of this book would have happened without you.

Index